Knowing the God of All Comfort

An Inductive Bible Study

Sunergos **Bible Studies**

Jan Wells

Copyright © 2023 by Jan Wells

Knowing the God of All Comfort – An Inductive Bible Study

Printed in the United States of America

ISBN 978-1-932934-10-6

Acknowledgments:

Scripture quotations are taken from the following:

Holman Christian Standard Bible, HCSB. Nashville, TN: Holman Bible Publishers, 2004.

The Holy Bible: English Standard Version, ESV. Wheaton, IL: Crossway Bibles, 2016.

The Holy Bible: International Standard Version, ISV. Yorba Linda, CA: The ISV Foundation; Davidson Press, Inc., 1999.

The New American Standard Bible, NASB. La Habra, CA: The Lockman Foundation, 1995. (www.Lockman.org)

Word studies are taken from James Strong's *The Comprehensive Concordance of the Bible*. Iowa Falls, IA: Word Publishing. When other sources are used in the center column of the word studies, they are printed in italics. A complete list of the references used for this study is found in the Bibliography.

Sunergos Bible Studies
2485 Morse Road
Sebastopol, CA 95472
707.829.2956

To order additional copies, visit www.*Sunergos*Bible.org

This study is dedicated to my dear husband, Richard and many dear friends who have shown me how to trust in God when facing grievous circumstances.

A special thank you to my dear friend, JulieAnn Smith who helped me finalize the formatting for this study!

I have written this Bible study that it might strengthen and encourage believers who are fellow workers, translated from the word **sunergos** in the New Testament Greek. We are to glorify God in all that we do, and the diligent study of His word will equip us to carry out God's plan in our life and in His church so that we might truly enjoy Him forever. Join with me that we might be fellow workers, allowing God's word to equip us as members of His body.

In His Love,

Jan

Jan Wells, M.A., Th. M.

email: jan@sunergosbible.org

website: www.sunergosbible.org

And we sent Timothy, our brother and God's fellow worker (*sunergo*), in the gospel of Christ, to strengthen and encourage you as to your faith, (1 Thessalonians 3:2).

I have found there are some prayers that I can voice that God will always answer. One is asking God to increase my desire to spend time with Him, asking Him that my spirit would long to commune with Him in the pages of His word. When you surrender your feeling of "you have to" study God's word, and instead ask God to help "you want to" spend time with Him, you will be delighted and amazed at the difference in your attitude toward the spiritual discipline of Bible study. *Sola Deo Gloria* (to God alone be the glory)!

Hymns are provided at the end of some of the sections of the study with the intention of leading to a time of worship. Having grown up in a church that used "hymns" for the worship service, I really appreciate the messages in Christian hymns that were written in the past.

Table of Contents

Table of Contents iv

Lesson 1 - Introduction to Knowing the God of All Comfort Study 7

God's Comfort Comes from His Truth – Psalms of Lament, and Expressing Words of Gratitude 7

   Introduction.. 7

     Days 1 and 2 – Introduction to the Study of "Knowing the God of All Comfort" 10

     Days 3 and 4 – God's Comfort Comes from the Truth of His Word.................................... 17

     Day 5 – A Look at the Psalms of Lament and Expressing Words of Gratitude 23

Lesson 2 – God's Comfort Comes from His Love and His Redemption - 29

Psalms of Lament, and Expressing Words of Gratitude 29

   Introduction... 29

     Days 1 and 2 – God's Comfort Comes through His Love and Compassion 29

     Days 3 and 4 – God's Comfort Comes through His Redemption and Salvation.................... 34

     Day 5 – A Look at the Psalms of Lament and Expressing Words of Gratitude 42

Lesson 3 – God's Comfort from His Faithfulness, His Power and Strength - 47

Psalms of Lament, and Expressing Words of Gratitude 47

   Introduction... 47

     Days 1 and 2 – God's Comfort Comes from His Faithfulness as He Is Trustworthy............ 47

     Days 3 and 4 - God's Comfort Comes through His Power and Strength 54

     Day 5 – A Look at Some Psalms of Lament and Expressing Words of Gratitude 59

Lesson 4 – God's Comfort Comes from His Wisdom and Peace – 63

Psalms of Lament, and Expressing Words of Gratitude 63

   Introduction... 63

     Days 1 and 2 – God's Comfort Comes from His Wisdom 63

     Days 3 and 4 – God's Comfort Comes from His Peace 68

     Day 5 – A Look at the Psalms of Lament and Expressing Words of Gratitude 72

Lesson 5 – Comfort Comes from Jesus, the Living Hope Who Brings Us Joy - 77

A Final Look at the Psalms of Lament, and Expressing Words of Gratitude 77

Introduction 77

Days 1 and 2 – God's Comfort Leads to Hope for Christ's Followers 77

Days 3 and 4 – God's Comfort Comes from the Joy We Have Because of Our Relationship with Him 85

Day 5 – Concluding Thoughts on God as the Comforter and How We Are to Comfort Others 92

APPENDIX 101

Personal Psalms of Lament 103

Lesson 1 - Introduction and Comfort Comes to Us from the Word of Truth 103

Lesson 2 - God's Comfort Comes to Us from His Love and Redemption 104

Lesson 3 - God's Comfort Comes to Us from His Faithfulness and His Power and Strength 105

Lesson 4 - God's Comfort Comes to Us from His Wisdom and Peace 106

Lesson 5 - God's Comfort Comes to Us from Jesus, the Living Hope Who Brings Us Joy 107

Gratitude Journal and Psalms of Thanksgiving 109

Inductive Study Methodology 113

Word Studies 119

Bibliography 121

Sunergos Bible Studies 123

Lesson 1 - Introduction to Knowing the God of All Comfort Study

God's Comfort Comes from His Truth – Psalms of Lament, and Expressing Words of Gratitude

Introduction

This topical study begins with the declarations made in 2 Corinthians 1:1-7 where v. 3 announces, "Blessed be the God and Father of our Lord Jesus Christ, the Father of mercies and God of all comfort." This study considers what the Apostle Paul meant by this statement, searching both the Old and New Testaments to see how those who believe in Jesus as Savior receive mercy and comfort from each member of the godhead. This study focuses on dimensions that provide care from the Triune God who minister whenever we are in need. Mercy and comfort are manifested in the following ways through God, the Father, Jesus, our Savior, and the Holy Spirit:

TRUTH,

LOVE,

REDEMPTION,

FAITHFULNESS,

POWER and STRENGTH,

WISDOM,

PEACE,

HOPE, and

JOY

On the other hand, in the midst of sorrow and sadness, Satan schemes to bring lies, anger and/or apathy, entanglement and slavery, thoughts of abandonment, weakness, foolishness, despair, and hopeless grief. Satan is the father of lies, (John 8:44) and he brings thoughts to deceive and confuse. God's mercy and comfort will quiet thoughts from Satan, our enemy. Scripture teaches that God brings mercy and comfort to those who are in any grievous struggle. God's comfort comes through His presence and His word. Paul said that "Christ in you" is the hope of glory, (Colossians 1:27). Our Savior Jesus taught that the Holy Spirit abides in believers, and will help and comfort us by guiding us into truth, (John 14:16; 16:13). The blood of Jesus has made it possible for us to have access before God's throne of grace so that in our time of need we receive mercy and grace, (Hebrews 4:16) from our loving heavenly Father. 1 John 4:4 declares a comparison between Jesus and the antichrist who comes against Him, saying, "greater is He who is in you, than he who is in the world."

In this study, Lesson 1 introduces key words in both the Old and New Testaments relating to comfort. Lesson 1 also opens with the first dimension of how we are comforted by each member of the godhead: by Scripture which represents God's truth. Each of the remaining lessons focus on two of the eight remaining dimensions of the Lord's mercy and comfort. The lessons teach how members of the godhead are revealed in Scripture in these specific ways:

1.) through the nature, identity, and ministry of each member of the godhead;

2.) by showing what God has done for us through His Son Jesus and through the Holy Spirit;

3.) by revealing what God is doing at the present time for those who believe; and

4.) by teaching how we are to respond to our heavenly Father, our Savior Jesus Christ, and the Holy Spirit.

The lessons also study the lives of individuals who turned to God for comfort as they grieved various forms of loss, disappointment, uncertainty and sorrow. We can benefit from studying these testimonies of humanity's response during grievous situations. Scripture provides evidence of the Lord's mercy and comfort. God directed men to record truths that have benefitted countless people over the centuries through the inspired words of Scripture.

At the end of each lesson, Day 5 focuses on specific psalms in Scripture identified as "Psalms of Lament" and how these psalms declare God's character relating to the themes of the lesson. The Psalms of Lament give us examples of how David and other psalmists (and prophets) "worked" out their grief, sorrow, and questions before God. Every Psalm of Lament is in (at least) two parts: words of lament, and declarations of who God is and His faithful nature. These laments will minister to your spirit regarding the many ways in which we are comforted by our God. You will be challenged to "write your own psalm of lament" to help you work through any situation that is on your heart, for yourself, someone you know and love, or the world in which you are living. Day 5 also encourages you to focus your mind on the ways you can express gratitude toward the Lord for His provision for you in the midst of every situation.

Paul wrote in 2 Timothy 3:16-17, "All Scripture is inspired by God and is useful for teaching, for reproof, for correction, and for training in righteousness, so that the person who belongs to God may be complete and thoroughly equipped for every good work." My prayer is that as you study these lessons you will believe that God's word is truly inspired, and through the Holy Spirit its message will be profitable for your own teaching, for your own reproof and correction, and for your own training in righteousness. God's word does equip His children for every good work. My prayer is that as you spend time in the word, you will learn more about God and His Son Jesus, so that your love for them will deepen and that you will be equipped by the faithful presence of the Holy Spirit for every circumstance that comes your way. This study is based on the following foundational truths that are held for those who follow Christ Jesus:

The Bible is the *holy and sacred* word of God.

The Bible is completely *inspired* by God.

The Bible is *inerrant*, which means it is *truthful* and *without error*.

The Bible is God's *revelation* of truth.

The Bible was written centuries ago and yet it is *relevant* for life today.

The Bible is God's *final authority* for all who follow Christ.

The Holy Spirit indwells believers and brings *illumination* to the study of the Bible.

The method of inductive study is used in this topical study "Knowing the God of All Comfort," in which the Bible is the primary source for information. The four components in inductive methodology include questions to help with the following:

1.) to carefully **observe** the text by looking to see what the text says;

2.) to accurately **interpret** the Scriptures which include some "historical" information, the context of the verse, and word studies to help you see what the text would have meant to its original audience;

3.) to determine the **eternal principles** in the text that have relevance today; and

4.) to **apply Scriptures** to the circumstances of the believer's life.

Each lesson studies portions of Scripture to bring understanding of what Scripture meant to the original audience as well as what it now means to those who follow Christ centuries later. Believers are to approach Scripture by being open to how the Holy Spirit reveals biblical truths. I have a friend who associates this process with "digging for potatoes," searching Scripture and expecting the Lord to reveal His truths in abundance for sustenance and nourishment. Another friend likens her time in the word to opening a box of chocolates, taking in and relishing the goodness of the Lord! In the discovery of biblical truths we gain insight into God's character and His purpose and plan for His children, as His light illuminates Scripture's sacred message.

We can praise the Lord for the provision of the Holy Spirit who guides believers into truth as mentioned earlier. Jesus promised His followers that the Holy Spirit helps believers understand the word. All believers have the same indwelling Holy Spirit to guide them into God's truth. When you feel frustrated or hear a voice telling you, "You cannot do this study," recognize that that thought is not coming from God. Our own flesh can defeat us and Satan devises a great many schemes to keep us from studying God's word. As you study, submit yourself to God, resist the devil, stand firm, and persevere. Trust God with how He will use His word to help you faithfully walk in a manner worthy of the gospel. For those who have placed their faith in Jesus Christ, the study of Scripture is a means to know more about God, one's Savior Jesus Christ, and the ministry of the Holy Spirit.

Days 1 and 2 – Introduction to the Study of "Knowing the God of All Comfort"

1.   When Paul opened his second letter to the church in Corinth, he used forms of the word "comfort" nine times in 2 Corinthians 1:3-7. What did Paul know about God that led him to testify in this way? Paul was a Jewish man who served as a Pharisee in the first century world. The Pharisees were students of God's word, and when Paul came to faith in Jesus, he learned about the person of Christ and Jesus' ministry as Savior. This study opens with Old Testament (OT) and New Testament (NT) truths that proclaim that God, Jesus, and the Holy Spirit each minister as merciful comforters. Open in **prayer** and we will then begin with several **observation questions** that always include one or more of the "5 W's and an H questions:" *who*, *what*, *where*, *when*, *why*, and *how*.

➤ <u>What</u> are the important declarations Paul makes about God and Christ in 2 Corinthians 1:3-7?

God: Christ:

➤ Paul used a "purpose clause" in 2 Corinthians 1:4, which is usually translated as "so that." <u>What</u> then is God's purpose for His children according to 2 Corinthians 1:4?

Paul said that those who follow Christ have been predestined to become conformed to the image of Christ in Romans 8:29. Studying Scripture provides a means for seeing Christ's character and the "image" in which we are to be conformed. Dr. M. Robert Mulholland wrote a very simple definition to describe "spiritual formation," when the Christian is "in the process of being conformed to the image of Christ for the sake of others." Allow God's holy word to be used to conform your life to the image of your Savior, Jesus. Allow God's word to transform you, so that it leads you to be all that God has created you to be. God intends for His children to be in fellowship with other believers. Romans 12:15 says we are "to weep or mourn with those who weep and rejoice with those who rejoice." Galatians 6:2 says we are "to bear one another's burdens."

➢ What does Hebrews 3:13 say about how we are to interact with others and why does it say this is important?

➢ What is said about believers and the church in Hebrews 10:22-25?

➢ What instructions are given in Hebrews 13:17 and why is this important?

➢ What does the psalmist write in Psalm 119:50 and Psalm 119:93 about God's word?

➢ A form of the same word Paul used in 2 Corinthians 1:3 is used by Jesus in His Upper Room Discourse when He described the person and ministry of the Holy Spirit. Read John 14:16 and John 14:26 and write out what Jesus declared about the Holy Spirit.

➢ What is said about mourning and comfort in Matthew 5:4?

➢ What does Jesus say we are to do when we are "weary and heavy laden," and what does Jesus say about Himself in Matthew 11:28-29? Elizabeth Elliott wrote, "Rest is a weapon given to us by God. The enemy hates it because he wants us to be stressed and occupied."

2.   In order to save the time of looking up words in reference books, **word studies** for **key words** are supplied in Question 2. Biblical scholars teach that the words used in Scripture often have many meanings and they seek to help determine how words were used by various authors, in various contexts, and in various situations. James Strong's concordance is a valuable resource for learning the meanings of words in the Bible.[1] The first column gives the Strong's number and the lexical form of the word, which is the word before it was changed grammatically to fit its context. The second line has the biblical reference for the word used in the lesson. The middle column gives definitions of the word from Strong's concordance and other references that are quoted in italics with the source footnoted, unless it is added from my research. The third column offers a cross-reference of the word from another passage. You might briefly summarize what you learn about the word from the cross-reference/s given, or just read the verse. Here are **word studies** for some **key words** in this part of the lesson.

Strong's # and Transliteration:	Definition from Strong's Concordance, unless written in italics:	Use of the word in other Scriptures:
3628 *oiktirmos* 2 Corinthians 1:3	**Mercies**, pity, compassion; *"display of concern over another's misfortune, pity, mercy, compassion"*[2]	Hebrews 4:16
7356 *raham* Lamentations 3:22	**Mercy,** by extension, the womb (as cherishing the fetus); by implication, a maiden: bowels, compassion, damsel, tender love, (great, tender) mercy, pity	Psalm 79:8
3874 *paraklesis* 2 Corinthians 1:3, 4, 6	**Comfort**, (noun), imploration, hortation, solace: consolation, exhortation, intreaty; *encouragement*	Acts 9:31
3870 *parakaleo* 2 Corinthians 1:4	**Comfort**, (verb), to call near, i.e. invite, invoke (by imploration, hortation or consolation): beseech, call for, (be of good) comfort, desire, (give) exhort (-ation), intreat, pray; to instill someone with courage or cheer	1 Thessalonians 3:2; 4:18; 5:11 2 Corinthians 2:7
3875 *parakletos* John 14:16	**Helper,** an intercessor, consoler: advocate, comforter; counselor.[3] *Used by John in John 14-16 and 1 John 2:1.*	John 14:26; 15:26; 16:7
5165 *nehamah* Psalm 119:50	**Comfort**, (noun), consolation. (Only used twice in the OT.)	Job 6:10

---

[1] James Strong, *The Comprehensive Concordance of the Bible* (Iowa Falls, IA: Word Publishing).

[2] Walter Bauer, Frederick W. Danker, William Arndt, and F. W. Gingrich, (hereafter BDAG), *A Greek-English Lexicon of the New Testament and Other Early Christian Literature* (Chicago, IL: University of Chicago Press, 2000), 700.

[3] This Greek word is associated with the legal system of the first century world, where a *paraklete* helped someone in a court of law. This *paraklete*, the Holy Spirit, is "another" helper alongside of Jesus. 1 John 2:1-2 says, Jesus is the *paraklete* with the Father and He is the propitiation for our sins.

Strong's # and Transliteration:	Definition from Strong's Concordance, unless written in italics:	Use of the word in other Scriptures:
2421 *chayah* Psalm 119:50	**Revive**, to live, whether literally or figuratively; . . . keep (leave, make) alive, certainly, give (promise) life, (let, suffer to) live, nourish up, preserve (alive), quicken, recover, repair, restore (to life), (God) save (alive, life, lives)	Psalm 119:93
5162 *nacham* Psalm 23:4	**Comfort**, to sigh, i.e. breathe strongly; by implication, to be sorry, i.e. (in a favorable sense) to pity, console or (reflexively) rue; or (unfavorably) to avenge (oneself): comfort (self), ease [one's self], repent (-er, -ing, self)	Psalm 86:17
3076 *lupeo* Ephesians 4:30	**Grief**, to distress; reflexively or passively, to be sad: cause grief, grieve, be in heaviness, (be) sorrow (-ful), be (make) sorry	2 Corinthians 7:8-9
3077 *lupe* 1 Peter 2:19	**Sorrows**, sadness: grief, grievous, grudgingly, heaviness, sorrow, sorrowful	Hebrews 12:11
4727 *stenazo* Hebrews 13:17	**Grief,** to make (be) in straits, i.e. (by implication) to sigh, murmur, pray inaudibly: . . . groan, grudge, sigh	2 Corinthians 5:2
2799 *klaio* Romans 12:15	**Weep**, to sob, i.e. wail aloud (whereas 1145 is rather to cry silently): bewail	Luke 6:21
3996 *pentheo* Matthew 5:4	**Mourn,** to grieve (the feeling or the act): mourn, (be-) wail	James 4:9

3.   In this introduction, we acknowledged the powerful truths and instructions given by Paul to his disciple Timothy in 2 Timothy 3:16-17. Paul gives the reasons for this. Read this passage and write out these reasons.

The Old Testament declares the "inspiration" of God's recorded word in David's psalm in 2 Samuel 23. Read what David wrote in 2 Samuel 23:2 and write out what David testified at the opening of his psalm.

David was also inspired to write Psalm 110 which became the most quoted Psalm in the NT, a message of the promised Messiah, critical to understanding the position of Jesus Christ. What is prophesied in Psalm 110 about the Messiah and what specifically does this say about Jesus? Before answering these questions read Jesus' words in Matthew 22:35-45. What does Jesus say about Psalm 110 and what does Jesus say about David?

4.   In the **observation questions**, you looked at Jesus' declarations about the coming of the Holy Spirit. This would have been very significant for His followers because in the time before Jesus coming, the Holy Spirit, generally called the Spirit of the Lord, would only anoint those who served God in a significant way, as a prophet or a king.[4] After Jesus returned to heaven, the Holy Spirit came to anoint all who believe in Jesus. Stop and meditate on this amazing gift God gives to His children when they accept Jesus as Savior.

What else did Jesus say about the Holy Spirit in the Upper Room Discourse?

a. John 14:17-18

b. John 15:26-27

c. John 16:7-15

---

[4] The angel Gabriel told Mary the mother of Jesus "the Holy Spirit will come upon you and the power of the Most High will overshadow you; and for that reason the holy offspring shall be called the Son of God," (Luke 1:35). Soon after this, Mary visited with Elizabeth, the mother of John the Baptist, and upon their greeting, "the baby leaped in her womb, and Elizabeth was filled with the Holy Spirit," (Luke 1:41).

5.   The information and questions "in the box" at the end of each lesson add to the theme of the day's focus and lead to practical application.

Grief can come from a variety of sources such as the following:

Grief can follow any traumatic event that brings change to one's life.

Grief comes to those who have lost a loved one to death, because when a loved one dies, circumstances dramatically change for those remaining.

Grief comes from difficult relationships where a connection is made with someone whose behavior does not change. An example of this would be a relationship with someone who has a mental illness that contributes to the instability of their behavior.

Grief can come from a change in one's health that requires changing one's lifestyle and/or focus. For example, losing one's hearing causes grief and calls one to address the loss and seek the medical care that can perhaps help with the situation.

Grief comes from the loss of a relationship with another person and while Jesus said be at peace with one another, Paul wrote, "as much as it is possible, live at peace with everyone," (Romans 12:18). Grief can come when it is not possible to live at peace with someone.

Grief can come from events that bring change, especially when one does not know how this situation will eventually unfold, as in the case of dementia, Alzheimer's disease, or the results of a traumatic brain injury.

Grief comes for a believer when someone you love walks away from the Lord or refuses to make a commitment to Jesus.

Grief comes from an unfulfilled dream, such as wanting to marry and have children and yet remaining single.

Grief can come from desiring something that someone else receives. This grief can lead to destructive jealousy.

Grief comes when a loved one goes through a trial of any sort.

Grief comes from the realities of how the aging process changes one's life.

Grief from any source can bring physical and emotional weariness and spiritual doubt. The process of grieving is hard work and moving through the grieving process requires determination, time, and faith that God's means of comfort are sufficient. We need comfort to help us when we grieve, because grief causes sorrow and sadness. Studies on the topic of grief have acknowledged "stages" one can go through in the grieving process. Elizabeth Kubler Ross published her research on the grieving process in the 1970's declaring the five dimensions of grief to be as follows:

1.) denial;
2.) anger;
3.) bargaining;
4.) depression; and
5.) acceptance.

In Iris Lin and Nhi Huynh's 2020 study on grief they developed the following seven stages of grief:

1.) shock and denial;
2.) pain and guilt;
3.) anger and bargaining;
4.) depression, loneliness, and reflection;
5.) an upward turn;
6.) reconstruction; and
7.) acceptance and hope.

Phillip Keller wrote an excellent book entitled, *A Shepherd Looks at Psalm 23* based on his experience with shepherds when he lived in South Africa as well as his experience with his God and his Savior, Jesus. Chapter 8 focuses on the phrase in Psalm 23:4, "Thy rod and Thy staff they comfort me."[5] In the world unfamiliar with the life of a shepherd, it is hard to understand why David wrote of his Shepherd, "His rod and His staff, they comfort me." The rod of the shepherd symbolizes his strength, his control, his authority, and his power, sometimes to lead and sometimes for discipline when the sheep "wander." The staff was/is used to lead the sheep as David declared in vv. 2-3. So in the context of all of Psalm 23, what exactly does David say about his LORD's role in his life that brings him comfort? (I have added Psalm 23 below for your reflection.)

As you move through this study, you will be challenged to make a commitment to the spiritual discipline of Scripture memorization by memorizing at least one verse from each lesson. This will minister to your spirit and equip you for difficult circumstances that come your way. You might struggle with memorizing verses from the Bible, but you must not give up or think that this is too difficult, because *it is possible* for all believers to treasure God's word in their heart and mind in this way. Trust that God will use His holy word to minister to your spirit. Scripture memorization will also equip you to share your faith with others.

---

[5] Phillip Keller, *A Shepherd Looks at Psalm 23* (Grand Rapids, MI: Zondervan Publishing House, 1982), 93-103.

Have you ever memorized Psalm 23? That might be a good challenge for you to help you reflect on the Lord, your comforter.

Let David's words be your prayer today as you close your time in God's holy word.

¹"The LORD is my shepherd, I shall not want.

²He makes me lie down in green pastures; He leads me beside quiet waters.

³He restores my soul; He guides me in the paths of righteousness for His name's sake.

⁴Even though I walk through the valley of the shadow of death, I fear no evil, for You are with me; Your rod and Your staff, they comfort me.

⁵You prepare a table before me in the presence of my enemies; You have anointed my head with oil; my cup overflows.

⁶Surely goodness and lovingkindness will follow me all the days of my life, and I will dwell in the house of the LORD forever," (NASB).

Days 3 and 4 – God's Comfort Comes from Truths in His Word

1.   The truths declared in the Bible about the identity and character of God, our heavenly Father, our Savior Jesus Christ, and the Holy Spirit can bring comfort to God's children. In these declarations we also learn of the promises that have been made, first to the nation of Israel and now to those who believe in Jesus.

The world apart from the Lord does not always have a passion for truth. Years ago the phrase was introduced about putting "a spin on" a story, whether it be news or history. For a variety of reasons people "stretched" the truth, "distorted" the truth, or perhaps "ignored" the truth. People who are critics of the Bible teach others that the Bible is not truth, and certainly not absolute truth. Those skeptical of the Bible seldom seek the truth found in its message. Open your time in the word in **prayer** and begin with these **observation questions**.

➤ David writes in Psalm 25:5 "Lead me in your truth and teach me, for you are the God of my salvation; for you I wait all the day long," (ESV). In Psalm 18:30, David declares "God, His way is perfect; the word of the LORD proves true; He is a shield for all those who take refuge in Him." Read Psalm 12 and summarize <u>what</u> David contrasts relating to "words" in Psalm 12.

➤ In the midst of trauma of any kind, stress can cause us to forget God's truths. Many times in Scripture we are told to "remember" and "not forget" God's word. We can learn from David's response to his difficult circumstances when he chose to not forget the benefits associated with knowing his God. David declared, "Praise the LORD, O my soul, and all that is within me, praise His holy name. Praise the LORD, O my soul, and forget not all His benefits," (Psalm 103:1-2). The psalmist of Psalm 119 declares of God's word, "Your word I have hid in my heart, that I might not sin against You," (Psalm 119:11). Read

Psalm 119:49-56 and then write out <u>what</u> the psalmist says about his commitment to the LORD in vv. 55-56. (Notice how v. 50 uses the word "comfort.")[6]

➤ Jesus was talking with some Pharisees about what it would mean to follow Him. In John 8:12, Jesus said "I am the light of the world. Anyone who follows Me will never walk in the darkness but will have the light of life." Jesus confronts the Pharisees by contrasting Himself with them, saying, "I am from above. You are of this world; I am not of this world," (John 8:23), and "the One who sent Me is true, and what I have heard from Him, these things, I tell the world," (John 8:26, HCSB). Jesus said to the Jews who believed in Him, "If you continue in My word, you really are My disciples. You will know the truth, and the truth will set you free," (John 8:31-32). <u>What</u> did Jesus say He meant by being "set free" according to John 8:34-36?

➤ Another significant teaching about truth is recorded in John 14, where Jesus testifies of His relationship with His Father and reveals the future for His followers. <u>What</u> does Jesus say in John 14:6 about Himself, His Father, and those who believe in Him?

➤ In Ephesians 6:10-20, Paul writes about a means God provides for His children to be "armored" against the schemes the enemy brings to us. To introduce this passage which is explored in a later question, <u>what</u> does Paul say about truth in Ephesians 6:14?

2.   Here are **word studies** for some **key words** in this part of the lesson.

Strong's # and Transliteration:	Definition from Strong's Concordance, unless written in italics:	Use of the word in other Scriptures:
571 *emeth* Psalm 25:5	**Truth**, stability; figuratively, certainty, truth, trustworthiness: assured (-ly), establishment, faithful, right, sure, true (-ly, -th), verity	Psalm 25:10

---

[6] In the OT, several words are used to represent God's truth: His word, His law, His precepts, His ordinances, and His commandments.

Strong's # and Transliteration:	Definition from Strong's Concordance, unless written in italics:	Use of the word in other Scriptures:
1697 *dabar* Psalm 106:12 (A historical prayer.)	**Word**, by implication, a matter (as spoken of) or thing; adverbially, a cause: act, advice, affair, answer, any such (thing), . . . chronicles, commandment, commune (-ication), concern [-ing], confer, counsel, . . . judgment, language, . . . message, oracle, . . . *revelation*	Deuteronomy 5:22 1 Kings 17:24
565 *imrah* Psalm 12:6	**Words**, commandment, speech, word. This is the feminine of *emer* (#561), something said: answer, appointed unto him, saying, speech, word	Psalm 18:30
2142 *zakar* Psalm 119:55	**Remember**, to mark (so as to be recognized), i.e. to remember; by implication, to mention	Psalm 77:11
225 *aletheia* John 8:32	**Truth**, true, truly, verity	John 14:6
3056 *logos* Hebrews 4:12	**Word**, something said (including the thought); reasoning (the mental faculty) or motive; . . . (with the article in John 1:1) the Divine Expression, speech, talk, treatise, utterance	Revelation 3:10
3403 *mimnesko* 2 Peter 3:2	**Remember**, to remind, i.e. to recall to mind, be mindful	Jude 17[7]

3.   1 Kings 17-19 and 2 Kings 1-2 tells of Elijah the prophet who was called to speak God's message of truth to the people of Israel. Elijah served when the northern kingdom of Israel was ruled by King Ahab who "did what was evil in the LORD's sight more than all who were before him," (1 Kings 16:30). Ahab married Jezebel who served the gods of Baal and rose up against God and His prophet Elijah.

The first recorded prophecy from Elijah was before King Ahab when the LORD declares there would be "no rain or dew during these years except by my command," (1 Kings 17:1). Read 1 Kings 17 to see how God provided for Elijah and how God provided for the widow of Zarephath that led to her testimony in 1 Kings 17:24, "Now I know that you are a man of God, and that the word of the LORD from your mouth is truth."

---

[7] Many times in the OT the phrase, "the word of the LORD came to. . . " was used in association with the prophets God sent to His people Israel. In the first century epistles we learn that the "words of the apostles" were also recognized as God's message to followers of Jesus, (as in 2 Peter 3:2 and Jude 17.)

Scripture records Elijah's struggles with depression because of the circumstances of his life and what was taking place in his beloved country. Read 1 Kings 18:17-46 to see what is revealed about God in this narrative.

Elijah was told to anoint Elisha as prophet in 1 Kings 19:16. Look at 2 Kings 2:1-14 to see how God revealed Himself to Elijah and Elisha and the fifty men who were witnesses.

Read Jesus' words in Luke 4:24-26 and summarize what was said about Elijah in this passage.

Looking at the context of James' mention of Elijah in James 5:17-18, what is the purpose for Elijah's mention? (Look at James 5:13-18 and think about the message the Holy Spirit had for all of the believers who received James' epistle.)

Take some time to stop and think about what you have learned about Elijah the prophet. What can we learn about how Elijah lived and what do the passages you studied teach you about the God he served?

4.   Paul writes about the spiritual armor in Ephesians 6. What are the commands introducing the armor according to Ephesians 6:10-11, 13a and what is the purpose for this armor according to Ephesians 6:11-13?

What has God provided for His children according to Ephesians 6:14-20 and to what is each piece of armor associated?

Read the opening of Isaiah 11 to see what is said about the coming Messiah and what is declared in Isaiah 11:5.

How did Paul interpret Isaiah 11:5 in his description of the armor God has given us?

5.   Read what David said in Psalm 12 about God's word and how he contrasted this to those who had not remained faithful in vv. 1-2.

What does David testify in Psalm 18:30 about God's word and what does this mean to those who "take refuge in Him"?

According to 1 John 4:1-6, what has God done for us so that we can know what compares to God's truth?

What did Paul write about Satan in 2 Corinthians 2:11 and what challenge does this bring to believers?

What is declared in 1 John 5:20 about both God and Jesus, and what that means to those who follow Jesus?

Remember in the opening of Psalm 103, David testifies of his intention to "Bless the LORD O, my soul, and all that is within me, bless His holy name." Bless the LORD, O my soul, and forget none of His benefits." You are searching for the "benefits" of our God and our Savior, and the Holy Spirit as you move through this study. May you truly be blessed as you reflect on the word of God that He has preserved over the centuries.

Paul wrote in Colossians 3:16, "Let the word of Christ richly dwell within you, with all wisdom teaching and admonishing one another with psalms and hymns and spiritual songs, singing with thankfulness in your hearts to God." Are you living in obedience to these commands? What in these commands is a challenge for you?

We can claim these truths and trust in Jesus' words, even though we might have questions and challenges that will come to us in life. We can search for truths that will lead us to God's comfort. As Paul directed believers to put on the armor of God, the first piece of the armor he mentioned was the belt of truth, and then in Ephesians 6:17 we are told to take up the sword of the Spirit, the word of God. Read what Hebrews 4:12-13 says about the word of God, and write out what these two verses declare.

Stop and think what this means to you and continue to read through the end of the chapter to see what is said about your relationship with God.

Think back over what you have studied in this portion of the lesson and choose a verse to meditate upon, so that you might remember its truth. You might memorize the verse about God's truth, so that it truly becomes your "sword of the Spirit," bringing strength and discernment to your soul.

"Open My Eyes"

Open my eyes, that I may see glimpses of truth Thou hast for me; place in my hands the wonderful key that shall unclasp and set me free.

Refrain: Silently now I wait for Thee, ready my God, Thy will to see; open my eyes illumine me, Spirit divine.

Open my ears, that I may hear voices of truth Thou sendest clear; and while the wave notes fall on my ear, everything false will disappear.

Refrain:

Open my mouth, and let me bear, gladly the warm truth everywhere; open my heart and let me prepare love with Thy children thus to share.

Refrain:

By Clara H. Scott

Day 5 – A Look at the Psalms of Lament and Expressing Words of Gratitude

1.   Every lesson concludes with a focus on biblical Psalms of Lament that confirm the means by which psalmist's were comforted by the Lord. Truthfully, in the Psalms of Lament, the psalmist often complains about what God has allowed and cries out to God, often in anger and anguish. I thought about the early church fathers and the Jewish rabbis who left the Psalms of Lament in the Christian canon as well as the Hebrew canon of Scripture. As I have been studying these Psalms of Lament, I have seen that the psalmists were "modeling" a process of grieving that is necessary for healing: when someone is grieving, they must be honest with themselves and move out of denial, and not deny how unresolved grief takes its toll on those who have not yet "worked through" the grieving process or even by denying that what has taken place isn't that significant.

        In the Psalms of Lament, the psalmists "process" their grief, which models how we can move toward healing by crying out to God in our frustration and perhaps asking questions of God, and then reminding ourselves of the nature and provision of our heavenly Father. The grieving process requires expressions of emotion, working through anger, resentment, and/or guilt. Depression, loneliness, and fear often stem from trauma, loss, and grief and these can cause physical responses to the circumstance. Working through one's grief is important for being able to move toward a healthy response in any grievous situation or loss. We can benefit from the testimonies of the psalmists as they respond to hardships and sorrow, sadness, and grief. Open your time in the word in **prayer** and begin with these **observation questions**.

➢ Ecclesiastes 3 presents teaching about "an appointed time for everything. And there is a time for every event under heaven," (Ecclesiastes 3:1). Read Ecclesiastes 3:2-8 and then write out <u>what</u> is taught about grief and <u>what</u> is contrasted with it in v. 4.

➢ <u>What</u> does Paul say in Romans 12:15 that agrees with the teaching in Ecclesiastes 3?

➢ The book of Lamentations was the prophet Jeremiah's response to his situation, inspired by the Holy Spirit so that we might benefit from its truths. Jeremiah witnessed the impact upon his people because of the destruction of the Temple in Jerusalem and the exile of many people into the captivity of the Babylonians. The book of Lamentations reflects the "lament" of the prophet Jeremiah before His LORD. Jeremiah said to God in Lamentations 3:22-26, "Remember my affliction, and my homelessness, the wormwood and the poison. I continually remember them and have become depressed. Yet I call this to mind, and therefore I have hope." <u>What</u> does Jeremiah declare of God in Lamentations 3:22-26?

➤ Read Lamentations 5:19-22 and write out Jeremiah's requests in Lamentations 5:21.

2.   Here are **word studies** for some **key words** in this part of the lesson.

Strong's # and Transliteration:	Definition from Strong's Concordance, unless written in italics:	Use of the word in other Scriptures:
5594 *caphad* Joel 1:13	**Lament**, properly, to tear the hair and beat the breasts (as Orientals do in grief); generally, to lament; by implication, to wail: mourn (-er)	Zechariah 12:10 (This is an important prophecy.)
5091 *nahah* Micah 2:4	**Lament,** to groan, i.e. bewail; hence (through the idea of crying aloud) to assemble (as if on proclamation): to wail	1 Samuel 7:2
5092 *nehiy* Micah 2:4	**Lamentation,** (from #5091) an elegy: wailing	Jeremiah 31:15 (This is quoted in Matthew 2:18, see below.)
2896 *towb* Psalm 25:8	**Good,** beautiful, best, better, bountiful, cheerful, at ease, favor, fine, glad, graciously, joyful, kindly, kindness	Psalm 86:5
3034 *yada* Psalm 28:7	**Thank,** especially to revere or worship (with extended hands): . . . (make) confess (-ion), praise, (give) thank (-ful, -s,- sgiving)	Psalm 92:1
8426 *towdah* Psalm 26:7	**Thanksgiving,** an extension of the hand, i.e. by implication, avowal, or (usually) adoration; specifically a choir of worshippers: confession, (sacrifice of) praise, thanks (-giving, offering)	Leviticus 7:12
2354 *threneo* John 16:20	**Lament,** (from #2355); to bewail: lament, mourn. *"To express oneself in sorrowful tones, mourn, . . . to express oneself in a song or hymn of grief, sing a dirge."*[8]	Luke 23:27
3602 *odurmos* Matthew 2:18	**Lamented,** moaning, lamentation, mourning	2 Corinthians 7:7
5485 *charis* evelation 1:4	**Grace,** graciousness (as gratifying), of manner or act (abstract or concrete; literal, figurative or spiritual; especially the divine influence upon the heart, and its reflection in the life; including gratitude); acceptable, benefit, favour, gift, joy, pleasure, thank (-s, -worthy)	Ephesians 2:8-9

---

[8] BDAG, Ibid., 458.

Strong's # and Transliteration:	Definition from Strong's Concordance, unless written in italics:	Use of the word in other Scriptures:
2169 *eucharistia* 2 Corinthians 9:11	**Thanksgiving**, gratitude, actively grateful language (to God, as an act of worship): thankfulness (giving of thanks (-giving)	2 Corinthians 1:11

3.   When looking at the **word studies** for "lament" and forms of the word, you see that lament involved a verbal expression, as some of the words literally mean "to cry aloud, to moan, and to wail." Because of how forms of the word "lament" are used in Scripture, I thought of the passage in Romans 8 that teaches us about the comforting role of the Holy Spirit when we don't know how to pray. Paul teaches about many dimensions of the ministry of each member of the Trinity in Romans 8:26-39. What are ten truths you need to remember from this passage about your God, your Savior, and the Holy Spirit?

4.   The closing questions in Day 5 focus on several ideas: first the reading and meditating on a biblical "Psalm of Lament," writing of your own "psalm of lament," and then focusing your mind on a response of gratitude and thanksgiving for what you know of God and His provision for you.

The reason I chose Psalm 25 for this first "Psalm of Lament" is because of what David says about God in Psalm 25:5 and 10. Write out these verses here and meditate on these truths.

Read all of Psalm 25 and notice where David "cries" out to God. In many of the "Psalms of Lament," the psalmist cries out at the beginning of the lament, and he then testifies of God's nature and character. Where do you see David bring his "lament" before God in Psalm 25?

Often times in a Psalm of Lament, the declarations about God relate to the struggle the psalmist is experiencing. These psalms "teach" us about who God is, as the Holy Spirit who inspired the psalm knew that individuals would hear the psalm being read and in fact would sing the words when the people of Israel gathered. The psalms reveal important theological teaching about God as well as instructions for His children to follow. David wrote in Psalm 26:2-3, "Examine me, O LORD, and try me; test my mind and my heart. For Your covenant love is before my eyes, and I have walked in Your truth." Then Psalm 26:7 says, "That I may proclaim with the voice of thanksgiving and declare all Thy wonders."

When you take the time to write your own psalm of lament it helps you process your grief, and in this process God brings comfort and that promotes healing. Your grief might be concerning your own circumstances, or those of a loved one, or in response to circumstances in your church, or in the world in which we live. We benefit from looking at the life stories in the Bible of men and women who knew God and believed in Him. What a comfort and encouragement to claim David's declaration of God, "The eyes of the LORD are on the righteous, and His ears are open to their cry for help," (Psalm 34:15)! Take some time and write out your own psalm of lament, before the Lord and your Savior Jesus Christ. Trust the ministry of the Holy Spirit to guide you, to comfort you, to help you express your grief as you write. While you are writing, reflect on truths about each member of the godhead and what this means to you. Write out your psalm of lament in the Appendix.

James 5:16 says, "Confess your sins to one another, and pray for one another, so that you may be healed. The effective prayer of a righteous person can accomplish much." Sharing your psalm of lament can connect you with another believer you can trust. If you do not have someone in your life that you can share with, ask God for a friend that can hold you accountable, a friend you can ask for prayer. Sorrow can emotionally drain your spirit, and yet believers are promised that comfort comes from God.

Grief leads to suffering from any loss. We cannot expect a grieving person to become their "old self" again, because in the process of grieving, a person comes out a "different" person, which can either make one stronger or sadly, weaker. Someone said that after they suffered a loss, they realized how important it was to journal the precious memories that were associated with their sorrow, to allow the memories and yet to not get "stuck" in the memories, but to work through what was special and a benefit to them.

Each "Day 5" for this study also reflects on truths about expressing gratitude toward God. In the Appendix, there is space for you to "list" ways in which you are grateful. A friend of mine was going through some grievous situations with several members of her family and she began the habit (initially by forcing herself) to think of five things she was thankful for at the end of each day. When she reflected on this list, it helped her face and process her sorrow and the fear of the unknown that accompanied her sorrow. In the Appendix, write out your own Psalm of Thanksgiving, expressing at least five ways in which you are thankful.

Close your time in prayer, meditating before the Lord, "the father of mercies and the God of all comfort," (2 Corinthians 1:3). In the Hebrew language the word "meditate" carried a verbal expression. Thus Psalm 1 teaches that a person is "blessed" when they delight in God's word, and when they meditate day and night (Psalm 1:2), in other words, talk to God and your Savior, Jesus. Allow the Holy Spirit to guide you into God's word that will always minister to your spirit. God is always open to our prayer since Jesus provided access to the throne of grace when He offered Himself on a horrible cross to die for our sin. This truth is God's truth, it is God's provision for His children and reflects His mercies and His comfort.

The other dimension of the biblical understanding of meditation being a verbal expression (based on the Hebrew word *hagah*), is to express to others what God means to you based on truths from the Bible. This sharing will help you testify of God's blessings as you journey through the process of your grief.

Lesson 2 – God's Comfort Comes from His Love and His Redemption -

Psalms of Lament and Expressing Words of Gratitude

Introduction

Days 1 and 2 of this lesson focus on God's love, His compassion, and His mercy, and then the focus of Days 3 and 4 is God's redemption and His salvation for those who believe in Jesus as Messiah. Day 5 continues to study some Psalms of Lament and the instructions in the Bible commanding us to be thankful and express our thankfulness before our God, the Father of mercies and the God of all comfort. Many times in the Psalms we read of the psalmists crying out to God and asking for His mercy, and this lesson continues our search for what is meant by God being a gracious and compassionate God.

Another attribute of God is His goodness. In the English language, forms of the word "good" seldom express the grandeur of our God's nature. When we are grieving, it can be difficult to reflect on God as a "good" God. As you move through this study, forms of the word "good" are explored as they relate to the nature of our loving heavenly Father.

Days 1 and 2 – God's Comfort Comes through His Love and Compassion

1.   Open your time in the word with a time of **prayer**, humbly coming before the Lord and seeking His help as you look into His holy word. Now begin with these **observation questions**.
  ➢ Many times Scripture passages contain several dimensions of God's character and His attributes. In Lesson 1 you read Psalm 23; read the psalm again today and write out Psalm 23:6. Take some time to meditate on what Psalm 23:6 means to you.

  ➢ The Psalms were sung by the nation of Israel when they met in the synagogues on the Sabbath after returning from exile, first by the Babylonians and then by the Persians. When the OT was translated into the Greek language, the book of Psalms was given the name "Psalms," which is the Greek word for "songs." A number of Psalms have been turned into songs that are sung today in the Christian church. The words of Psalm 36:5-7 have been put to music (in English) today. What does David say about God in Psalm 36:5-7? (Notice the first character quality that David declared of his God.)

  ➢ Read God's message in Deuteronomy 7:7-12 about His relationship with Israel before they were to enter the land He had promised them. What does God say about Israel in this passage? (Notice in the **word studies** the three words for love used in this passage.)

➢ The love of God is associated with the covenant God made with His people. God's covenant with Abram (before his name was changed to Abraham) is revealed in Genesis 15. In the ancient world, a covenant was "formalized" with the shedding of blood, and in Genesis 17 God said that circumcision was to be the symbol of His covenant with His people, Israel (Genesis 17:13). The Ten Commandments God gave to Israel were called the "words of the covenant" (Exodus 34:28). Jeremiah and Ezekiel prophesied about the new covenant that was to come. Read Jeremiah 31:31-34 and Ezekiel 36:22-29 and summarize <u>what</u> is promised in these passages. (Remember what Jesus said about the role of the Holy Spirit in His Upper Room Discourse in John 14 and 16 that you studied in Lesson 1.)[9]

➢ <u>What</u> is said about mercy in Matthew 5:7?

➢ In response to the conversation Jesus had with Nicodemus, <u>what</u> did Jesus say about God's love in John 3:16-17?

2.   Here are **word studies** for some **key words** in this part of the lesson.

Strong's # and Transliteration:	Definition from Strong's Concordance, unless written in italics:	Use of the word in other Scriptures:
2617 *checed* Psalm 13:5	**Lovingkindness**, kindness, by implication (towards God), subjectively beauty, merciful, mercy, pity; considered as a "divine attribute;" *steadfast love, covenant love*	Psalm 136:1-26 (In every verse.)
2836 *chashaq* Deuteronomy 7:7	**Love,** to cling, i.e. join, (figuratively) to love, delight in; . . . (have a) desire	Deuteronomy 10:15

---

[9] Jesus told His disciples at the first Lord's Supper that the wine He served represented "the new covenant in My blood," (Luke 22:20), and Matthew 26:28 records Jesus saying, "My blood of the covenant." Hebrews testifies of Jesus as the mediator of the new covenant, (Hebrews 8:6) and how Jesus' willingness to offer Himself brought cleansing and redemption, (Hebrews 9:14-15).

Strong's # and Transliteration:	Definition from Strong's Concordance, unless written in italics:	Use of the word in other Scriptures:
160 *ahabah* Deuteronomy 7:8	**Love,** (feminine form of love), see definition of word #157 below	Isaiah 63:9
157 *ahab* Deuteronomy 7:9	**Love,** to have affection for (sexually or otherwise): (be-) love (-d, -ly, -r,) like, friend	Deuteronomy 10:18
2603 *chanan* Psalm 6:2	**Mercy,** to bend or stoop in kindness to an inferior; to favor, bestow; to implore (i.e. move to favor by petition): . . . (be, find, shew) favor, . . . (be) merciful, have (show) mercy (on, upon), have pity upon, pray; *to be gracious*	Psalm 123:3
1285 *beriyth* Genesis 17:19	**Covenant,** (in the sense of cutting), a compact, made by passing between pieces of flesh, confederacy, league	Jeremiah 31:31
8416 *tehillah* Isaiah 63:7	**Praiseworthy,** laudation, (concretely), a hymn, praise	Psalm 47:6, 7
7356 *racham* Isaiah 63:7	**Compassion,** see the **word study** for mercy in Lesson 1	Psalm 79:8
7320 *rob* Psalm 5:8	**Abundance,** abundantly, excellent, great (-ly, -ness, number), most, much, plenty, (-fully)	Psalm 106:45
25 *agapao* John 3:16	**Love,** to love (in a social or moral sense): (be-) love (-ed). *To want the best for someone.*	Romans 8:37
1656 *eleos* Hebrews 4:16	**Mercy,** compassion (human or divine, especially active): (tender) mercy	Titus 3:5
26 *agape* Romans 8:35	**Love,** affection or benevolence, specifically, a love feast: (feast of) charity (-ably), dear	John 15:9
1242 *diatheke* Luke 22:20	**Covenant,** a disposition, a contract (especially a devisory will); testament	Hebrews 8:6
5485 *charis* Ephesians 2:8-9	**Grace,** see the **word study** for grace in Lesson 1	Hebrews 4:14-16

3.   Look at these Scriptures to see how God's love and Christ's love are described.

  a. Psalm 5:8

b. 2 Corinthians 13:11

c. John 15:9-17

4.   Now please take the time to write out the qualities of God declared by David in Psalm 145:7, 8. (Verse 8 is taken from when God testifies of Himself to Moses in Exodus 34:6-7 and these words are also repeated several other places in the OT.)

Many times the Bible describes God without specifically saying He is a loving God. Psalm 23 is an example of this. Israel came to know God as the Shepherd who cared for them from David's 23rd Psalm. Ezekiel 34 opens with a message God gave to Ezekiel for the "shepherds" of Israel by speaking a "Woe to the shepherds of Israel" because they were not being faithful to their calling, but were taking care of themselves instead of the people under their care (Ezekiel 34:1-10). What does God promise to do among His people as their shepherd in Ezekiel 34:11-31? (Keep in mind, the nature of biblical prophecy is that some of the words of prophecy were fulfilled soon after they were given, some of the prophecies took place years, even hundreds of years later, and some of the prophecies in our Bible have yet to take place. Sometimes in a passage of prophecies, we can find each of these examples of the mysterious nature of God's timing. A unique Hebrew construction is found in Ezekiel 34:24 when God mentioned David. This phrase is in a "construct" grammatical form and could be translated as "My servant of David," which helps us understand the prophetic message God is delivering concerning the coming of Jesus, the Messiah.)

5.   What does Jesus say about Himself in John 10:11 and what does Jesus say this means in the context of the verse?

6.   Right before God prophesied to Jeremiah about the "new covenant" that would be coming, He told Jeremiah "I have loved you with an everlasting love, therefore I have drawn you with lovingkindness," (Jeremiah 31:3). After Israel returned from exile, the Holy Spirit inspired Psalm 136 as a reminder of God's *checed* (lovingkindness and/or covenant love) toward His people. Some psalms are written as "historical psalms" to remind the people of

Israel of God's love and His faithfulness. Write out the phrase that ends every verse in Psalm 136.

What is said about God in Psalm 136:23?

What is asked of us in Psalm 136:26?

I have been thinking about Psalm 136 and its message that the Holy Spirit wanted Israel to remember. Maybe we should all write a "historical psalm" in a similar format as Psalm 136 to reflect on our life and God's faithfulness. I remember a dear friend sharing with me after I had lost a close friend, that I should reflect on the precious memories created from our friendship and be thankful for the blessings of our friendship. In the pattern of Psalm 136, how would you acknowledge what God has done in your life in the past year?

God "speaks" comfort to us through His word, so memorizing Scripture can minister to our soul whenever we are in need. I challenge you to memorize a verse about God's love that you can claim as truth. You can write out the verse here.

The song "The Love of God" is Fredrick Lehman's response to Scripture. If you know the words you can sing this hymn or read the words as you reflect on God's love.

> ### "The Love of God"
>
> *The love of God is greater far than tongue or pen can ever tell; it goes beyond the highest star, and reaches to the lowest hell; the guilty pair, bowed down with care, God gave His Son to win; His erring child He reconciled, and pardoned from his sin.*
>
> *Refrain: Oh, love of God, how rich and pure! How measureless and strong! It shall forevermore endure, the saints' and angels' song.*
>
> *When hoary time shall pass away, and earthly thrones and kingdoms fall, when men who here refuse to pray, on rocks and hills and mountains call, God's love so sure, shall still endure, all measureless and strong; redeeming grace to Adam's race, the saints' and angels' song.*
>
> *Refrain:*
>
> *Could we with ink the ocean fill, and were the skies of parchment made, were every stalk on earth a quill, and every man a scribe by trade; to write the love of God above, would drain the ocean dry; nor could the scroll contain the whole, though stretched from sky to sky.*
>
> *Refrain:*
>
> By Frederick Lehman

Days 3 and 4 – God's Comfort Comes through His Redemption and Salvation

1.   When we are grieving the loss of a loved one, we can have GREAT solace if the person had a faith in Jesus as their Savior. When this is not the case, the pain of the loss is GREATLY magnified. We know that Peter acknowledged the heart of God in 2 Peter 3:9 by saying, "The Lord is not slow about His promise, as some count slowness, but is patient toward you, not wishing for any to perish but for all to come to repentance." God gives everyone a choice, and the free will to come to Him. This portion of the lesson looks first at the understanding of salvation and redemption as understood by the people of Israel before the coming of Jesus, the Messiah and then what is taught about salvation and redemption through Jesus. Acts 4:12 declares "There is salvation in no one else; for there is no other name under heaven that has been given among men, by which we must be saved."

        A beautiful Christmas carol was written by referencing the story of Simeon recorded in Luke 2:25-35. We are told that Simeon was in the temple when Mary and Joseph presented Jesus for circumcision (Luke 2:21). Simeon "was looking forward to the consolation of Israel, and the Holy Spirit was on him," (Luke 2:25). The word "consolation" is *paraklesis*, which can also be translated as comfort or solace. Open by reading or singing the words of this Christmas carol and allow the words to minister to your spirit in worship.

> *"Come, Thou Long-Expected Jesus"*
>
> *Come, Thou long expected Jesus, born to set Thy people free; from our fears and sins release us; let us find our rest in Thee.*
>
> *Israel's strength and consolation, hope of all the earth Thou art; dear desire of every nation, joy of every longing heart.*
>
> *Born Thy people to deliver, born a child and yet a king. Born to reign in us forever, now Thy gracious kingdom bring.*
>
> *By Thine own eternal Spirit rule in all our hearts alone; by Thine all sufficient merit, raise us to Thy glorious throne.*
>
> By Charles Wesley and Rowland H. Prichard

Open in a time of **prayer**, seeking God's help as you come before Him in His holy word and begin with these **observation questions**.

➤ David wrote Psalm 3 as his prayer before *Yahweh* and he mentioned several of the words associated with salvation for the people of Israel: deliverance (v. 2); save (v. 7); and salvation (v. 8). <u>What</u> is associated with these words within their context in Psalm 3?

➤ David testifies in Psalm 27:1, "*Yahweh* is my light and my salvation - whom should I fear? *Yahweh* is the stronghold of my life of whom should I be afraid?" Psalm 34:22 testifies of *Yahweh* who "redeems the life of His servants, and all who take refuge in Him will not be punished." Nahum 1:7 also presents a reminder of Israel's God. Write out this verse that uses the same Hebrew word "refuge," as David used in Psalm 34:22.

➤ Read Psalm 103:4-22 to see what David says about God's love and redemption. OT scholar Bruce Waltke studied the concept of fearing *Yahweh*, as the phrase "the fear of *Yahweh*" is used in the OT. He said the idea is to submit oneself to a sovereign God as if you were on your knees bowing before Him, while waving a white flag of surrender. Name five truths about God from this psalm including <u>what</u> is said in vv. 4 and 19.

➢ Isaiah was given many prophecies about the coming Messiah. Read Isaiah 61:1-2 and Isaiah 42:6-7 and then read what Jesus said in the synagogue in Nazareth at the beginning of His ministry in Luke 4:14-21. <u>What</u> did Jesus declare about His ministry and <u>how</u> did He testify of the fulfillment of these prophecies?

➢ Several places in the NT, Jesus speaks the words, "your sins are forgiven," (Mark 2:5; Luke 7:48). Jesus is the fulfillment of the new covenant as He taught in the first Lord's Supper about "the new covenant in My blood" in Luke 22:20. When Jesus was crucified His blood was shed for the forgiveness of sin. <u>What</u> does Hebrews 8:6 say about Jesus' ministry and the new covenant?

➢ <u>What</u> is said about Jesus in these verses?

     a. Romans 5:8-10

     b. Hebrews 2:14

     c. Hebrews 9:14-15

2.   Here are **word studies** for some **key words** in this part of the lesson.

Strong's # and Transliteration:	Definition from Strong's Concordance, unless written in italics:	Use of the word in other Scriptures:
3467 *yasha* Psalm 3:7	**Save**, to be open, wide or free, i.e. (by implication) to be safe; . . . defend, deliver (er), help, preserve, rescue, bring (having) salvation, get victory	Psalm 28:9; 6:4; 34:6, 18

Strong's # and Transliteration:	Definition from Strong's Concordance, unless written in italics:	Use of the word in other Scriptures:
3444 *yeshuwah* Psalm 3:2, 8	**Salvation**, something saved, i.e. (abstractly) deliverance, hence aid, victory, prosperity: health, help (-ing), save, saving (health), welfare	Exodus 15:2
5546 *callach* Psalm 86:5	**Forgive,** (an adjective from #5545), placable, ready to forgive	A *hapax legomen*. (The only place this word was used in the OT.)
6960 *qavah* Psalm 130:5	**Wait,** to bind together (perhaps by twisting), i.e. collect (figuratively), to expect: gather together, lock, patiently tarry, wait (for, on, upon)	Isaiah 40:31
5545 *calach* Jeremiah 31:34	**Forgive,** to forgive, pardon, spare; *forgiveness*	Exodus 34:9
5547 *celiychah* Psalm 130:4	**Forgiveness,** (from #5545) pardon; *abundant forgiveness*[10]	Nehemiah 9:17
6304 *peduth* Psalm 130:7	**Redemption,** distinction, also deliverance, division, redeem	Psalm 111:9
1350 *ga'al* Psalm 77:15	**Redeemed,** (according to the Oriental law of kinship), i.e. the next of kin, . . . to deliver, to purchase, to ransom	Jeremiah 31:11
863 *aphiemi* Matthew 6:12, 14-15	**Forgive,** to send forth, in various applications (as follow): . . . forsake, lay aside, leave, let (alone, be, go, have), omit, put (send) away, remit, suffer, yield up	Matthew 9:6
859 *aphesis* Luke 4:18	**Release,** (from #863, see above), freedom, i.e. pardon, deliverance, forgiveness, liberty, remission	Matthew 26:28
629 *apolutrosis* Romans 3:24	**Redemption,** (the act) ransom in full, i.e. figuratively, riddance, or specifically, i.e. Christian salvation, deliverance. *Originally, "buying back" a slave or captive, i.e. "making free" by payment of a ransom.*[11]	Ephesians 1:7

3.   From the very beginning, God has always given people free will. Sin entered the world because of the disobedience of Adam and Eve who opened the way for all of humanity to experience disease and death. In the OT, God was known as the Redeemer and the Deliverer of His people in the physical realm, as they were being saved and delivered from their enemy or from any danger. The Hebrew word for salvation, *yeshuwah,* had a physical connotation, and the

---

[10] Francis Brown, Samuel Rolles Driver, and Charles Augustus Briggs, [hereafter BDB], *Enhanced Brown-Diver-Briggs Hebrew and English Lexicon* (Oxford, UK: Clarendon Press, 1977), 699.

[11] BDAG, Ibid., 117.

literal meaning, "*Yahweh* saves." God was acknowledged as the One who delivered, rescued, and saved Israel as a nation. The first place the word appears in the OT is in Jacob's words to his sons, "For Your salvation, I wait, O the LORD" in Genesis 49:18. Moses spoke words of encouragement to Israel at the bank of the Red Sea before God fully promised their redemption from their slavery in Egypt, declaring, "Do not fear! Stand by and see the salvation of the LORD which He will accomplish for you today," (Exodus 14:13). In Moses' song of response to God's release from slavery in Egypt and the parting of the Red Sea, how did Moses open his song in Exodus 15:2?

What is said in Nehemiah 9:17b about God in the Levite's prayer of Nehemiah 9?

What is said about the LORD in Psalm 34:18?

4.   What is promised in God's prophecy to Jeremiah about the coming of the new covenant and the indwelling Holy Spirit according to these verses?

   a. Jeremiah 31:13

   b. Jeremiah 31:14

   c. Jeremiah 31:17

   d. Jeremiah 31:31-34

5.   After Israel returned from their exile in Persian captivity, a number of psalms were written. Among these is Psalm 130 which is called a Psalm of Ascents, intended to be sung as the people ascended the hill to the Temple in Jerusalem, to enter into worship. Read Psalm 130 to see how the psalmist uses these words.

    a. Forgiveness, in v. 4

    b. Redemption, in v. 7

    c. Redeem, in v. 8

    Another important truth in Psalm 130 is the psalmist's response to the LORD. Write out v. 5 and meditate on this testimony.

    The word "wait" in Psalm 130:5 is the same word that is used in Isaiah 40:31. Read the promise in Isaiah's testimony and then look back at the **word study** for the word "wait" to see the meaning of this Hebrew word. How does this promise challenge you and your response to God in the midst of difficulties?

6.   Genesis 37 - 50 reveals the life and struggles that Joseph had. Joseph was mistreated by his brothers, he was sold into slavery in Egypt, and was then imprisoned by being falsely charged by Potiphar's wife. Look at the heart of Joseph in Genesis 50. What does Joseph say in Genesis 50:19-21 to his brothers about God and how did his words impact his brothers?

Have you ever had a "Joseph moment" in your life? When you look back at this event or circumstance, how did God use this to bring you His "good"?

7.   What is declared about salvation in these NT verses and passages and what do these passages mean to you?

      a. John 3:16-17

      b. 1 Tim. 1:15-17

      c. Ephesians 1:13-14

8.   Paul described the ministry of Jesus in Romans 3:21-25 to help the people of the Roman Empire understand the gospel. Read these verses and meditate on the power of the gospel and God's gift to us.

In the first century world the word "gospel" meant "good news, the enemy has been conquered," from the time when Alexander the Greek was conquering the known world. The three realms of salvation are presented by Paul as follows:

1.) We are justified, in the legal realm, this meant you stand guilty before the judge in authority and yet he declares you are innocent;

2.) We have redemption, a word associated with the slave market where one is ransomed and set free; and

3.) In the religious first century world, atonement is made to appease the wrath of a god, and in the case of Christianity, the wrath of God has been removed by the blood of Christ. Jesus is the true Redeemer.

Read about Simeon in Luke 2:25-35 and Anna in Luke 2:36-38 to see what is said about the baby Jesus who was brought to the Temple to be circumcised.

9.   Sometimes our grief comes because someone has wounded us physically or emotionally. The nature of our flesh is to retaliate, but for those who follow Jesus, we are called to forgive those who have wronged us or our loved ones. We forgive to remove the enslavement to bitterness and revenge. For this healing we turn to Jesus, the author and finisher of our faith. We forgive and then we are to process the grief the event or circumstances have caused.

James Kimmel teaches about the problems that come from retaliation, which is the focus of his website www.savingcain.org where Dr. Kimmel acknowledges the power behind "revenge cravings." Everett Worthington teaches about the necessity to forgive and the error in thinking that "forgiveness is a process." Forgiveness is an act of obedience to the word of God, (Matthew 6:12, 14-15; Ephesians 4:32), and the circumstance that brought our grief calls us to "process our grief" to promote healing. As has been introduced, this processing of one's grief is modeled in the Psalms of Lament where the psalmist cries out to God while reminding himself of God's nature, so as to remember God's faithfulness.

There were three ways forgiveness was understood in the first century world and each holds the idea of "releasing," as explained in the Bible:

1.) To be released from debt, Luke 7:41-50; Matthew 18:21-35;

2.) To be released from slavery, John 8:34-36; Romans 3:24; 6:6-7, 17-18, 22-23; Galatians 5:1; and

3.) To be released from prison, Romans 7:22-25.

Jesus as our Redeemer has released those who believe in Him from a debt we could never pay, from slavery to sin, and from the prison of our sins. Praise God, we have been forgiven through Jesus' offering of Himself, as Jesus was our sinless, blameless sacrifice. As we are commanded to forgive others (Ephesians 4:32), Jesus empowers His followers to forgive when we have been wronged, and obedience to this brings freedom.

On the other hand, unforgiveness leads to bitterness and blocks the paths to healing and wholeness. We have been forgiven, we have been released, and yet unforgiveness in our hearts brings enslavement to sin. Jesus came to set us free according to John 8:32 and Galatians 5:1. Jesus said the thief comes to "rob, kill, and destroy" and He then declared that He has come that we might have life and might "have it abundantly," (John 10:10). This life represents living in the promises of God and working out our salvation in fear and trembling, (Philippians 2:12). Our enemy, Satan, comes against us and robs us of the comfort that God brings.

Sometimes grief comes from our own sin. We are told to confess our sin to one another and we will be healed, (James 5:16). Confession means to "agree" with the one in authority over us. Our God is a forgiving God and when we confess our sin, He is faithful and righteous to forgive us of our sin, and cleanse us from all unrighteousness, (1 John 1:9). When we sin we also need to forgive ourselves and apologize if another person was involved. Read the context of James 5:16 to see what James was directed to write concerning suffering and healing in James 5:13-17.

Think back to the many Scriptures you studied in this portion of the lesson. You might choose to memorize a verse that would contribute to your understanding of God's comfort and write it out here.

As those who follow Jesus, we acknowledge His ministry of redemption that He brought to those who believe. You might know the song "Redeemed" that expresses our redemption by the blood of the Lamb. Close by reading these words or singing this as a time of worship before Jesus, your worthy Savior.

"Redeemed"

Redeemed – how I love to proclaim it! Redeemed by the blood of the Lamb! Redeemed thru His infinite mercy, His child, and forever, I am.

Refrain: Redeemed, redeemed, redeemed by the blood of the Lamb; redeemed, redeemed, His child, and forever I am.

Redeemed and so happy in Jesus, no language my rapture can tell; I know that the light of His presence with me doth continually dwell.

Refrain:

I think of my blessed Redeemer, I think of Him all the day long; I sing, for I cannot be silent; His love is the theme of my song.

Refrain:

I know I shall see in His beauty, the King in whose law I delight; Who lovingly guardeth my footsteps, and giveth me songs in the night.

Refrain:

By Fanny Crosby and William J. Kirkpatrick

Day 5 – A Look at the Psalms of Lament and Expressing Words of Gratitude

1.   This lesson ends with a time of reflection upon several Psalms of Lament to see what was brought before God by David and the psalmist Asaph. Open your time in the word in **prayer**, seeking God's wisdom as you read so that you might see the message God has for you in His holy word. Open with these **observation questions**.

➢ In Psalm 13, one of David's Psalms of Lament, he testifies that he has trusted in God's *chesed*, which you will remember is an important word with several meanings, including mercy, lovingkindness, covenant love, and/or steadfast love. In Psalm 13:5 David testifies, "my heart shall rejoice in Your salvation." Read Psalm 13 to see the questions David brought before His God in vv. 1-2. <u>What</u> does David say is at stake in vv. 3-4?

➢ Psalm 77 is considered another Psalm of Lament that opens with a testimony by the psalmist, Asaph. <u>What</u> statement is introduced at the end of Psalm 77:1 that testifies of the psalmist's understanding of God?

➢ <u>What</u> are some of the concerns that Asaph declares in Psalm 77:2-9?

➢ At the end of Psalm 77:9 we see the word "*selah*," which is a word with debated meaning. Most biblical scholars interpret the word "*selah*" to mean a pause for silence and/or a musical interlude. Looking ahead to vv. 10-20, <u>what</u> role do you think the word "*selah*" takes in Psalm 77:9?

➢ <u>What</u> did Asaph promise in Psalm 77:11-12?

➢ <u>What</u> ministered to Asaph and helped him according to his Psalm of Lament?

2.   Here are **word studies** for some **key words** in this part of the lesson.

Strong's # and Transliteration:	Definition from Strong's Concordance, unless written in italics:	Use of the word in other Scriptures:
2490 *chalal* Psalm 77:10	**Grief**, to bore, i.e. (by implication) to wound, to dissolve; figuratively, to profane (a person, place or thing), to break (one's word), to begin (as if by an "opening wedge"); to pierce	Isaiah 53:5 (Of the Messiah.)
5945 *elyown* Psalm 77:10	**Most High**, (adjective) lofty (comparatively); as title, the Supreme: (Most, on) high (-er, -est), upper (-most)	Psalm 50:14

3.   As Asaph described God's redemption of Israel from Egypt in Psalm 77:10-20, I thought of the testimony of Rahab of Jericho, in the book of Joshua. What does this story in Joshua 2 and Joshua 6:22-27 reveal to you about God and what do you learn about Rahab in these passages?

Another reference to Rahab is found in the genealogy that Matthew recorded to introduce Jesus in Matthew 1. Something truly unique is presented in Matthew 1:4-6 that reveals the heart of God. (The genealogies of Israel were focused on the fathers, their sons, their grandsons, their great grandsons, etc.) What did the Holy Spirit direct Matthew to declare in this portion of the genealogy of Jesus?

Another confirmation of these truths is recorded in the genealogy at the end of the book of Ruth. This is evidence of the importance of the record of the "line of David," and those who followed in the tribe of Judah. What was recorded in Ruth 4:20-21 that is in agreement with Matthew's genealogy? (When you study the book of Ruth, you see Boaz, the son of Rahab and his character and obedience to God's law, which is further evidence of the heart of God.)

4.   The psalmist testifies in Psalm 118:28-29, "You are my God, and I give thanks to You. You are my God, I extol You. Give thanks to the LORD, for He is good; for His lovingkindness is everlasting." What does the psalmist Asaph promise in Psalm 50:14-15 and how is God identified in v. 14?

The Psalms of Lament demonstrate how we can relate to God in a variety of circumstances, in good times as well as in times of struggle. Roughly half of the 150 Psalms are Psalms of Lament. The Psalms of Lament follow a "pattern" with one exception, (Psalm 88). According to biblical scholars the Psalms of Lament follow this pattern: 1.) An intnroductory call for help; 2.) A complaint; 3.) An expression of confidence and trust; 4.) A petition and request; 5.) An assurance of being heard; and 6.) A commitment to praise.[12]

Psalm 88 is actually unique among all the Psalms of Lament because it does not end with "a vow of praise," but rather a lament with the last word "darkness." (in the Hebrew). In the book *The Problem of Pain*, C. S. Lewis writes "God whispers to us in our pleasures, speaks in our conscience, but shouts in our pains: it is [God's} megaphone to rouse a deaf world."[13] We can live in faith believing Romans 8:28, which declares, "We know that all things work together for the good of those who love God: those who are called according to His purpose."

Write out your own psalm of lament in the Appendix, perhaps including your struggles with some of the themes the lessons have studied: God's truth, His love, and the redemption that came through the blood of Christ Jesus.

As you close, continue recording your thoughts in the Appendix that express your gratitude to God for His love and His salvation. You might take some time to think about a time in your life when God made known to you His wonder and glory, His strength and faithfulness and provision for you, personally. Write out your response to the manifestation of God in your life, reflecting on His love and His redemption.

One way to focus on a passage of Scripture is through prayer. A method using three words that begin with the letter "R" has been suggested as a way of praying with a purpose through a passage of the Bible, and this helps make Scripture a living and powerful reminder of God's faithfulness. As you look back at Psalm 88, ask the Lord how you can REJOICE even in its truths, and then pray through these verses, rejoicing in the Lord our God and in your Savior Jesus Christ.

---

[12] Herman Gunkel and J. Begrich, *Introduction to the Psalms: The Genre of the Religious Lyric of Israel*, trans. J.D. Nogalski (Macon, GA: Mercer University Press, 1998), 177-186.

[13] C. S. Lewis, *The Problem of Pain* (The Centenary Press: UK, 1940), 93.

Look at Psalm 88 again to see how the Holy Spirit would lead you to REPENT concerning a struggle you have had relating to truths recorded in this psalm. Sometimes the biggest struggle is to have faith in our Lord and believe in His holy word. I think of the father who came to Jesus on behalf of his son and asked Jesus for help. Jesus responded by saying "Everything is possible to the one who believes," and the man responded by saying "I do believe! Help my unbelief," (Mark 9:24). Ask the Holy Spirit to reveal to you any area in Psalm 88 which leads you to REPENT.

The third "R" is for REQUEST, to be led by the Lord to REQUEST something, perhaps relating to the truths in this passage for yourself or for someone you know, or on behalf of your church, your community, or the world.

At a Youth for Christ rally when I was twelve years old, I heard the message of the gospel and was singing the song "Just As I Am" when I "went forward" and entrusted my life to Jesus. This song always reminds me of that decision I made. I am so thankful that I attended that Saturday evening service, where I surrendered my life to Jesus. You might let your closing prayer be led by the words of this song.

"Just As I Am"

Just as I am without one plea, but that Thy blood was shed for me, and that Thou bidd'st me come to Thee, O Lamb of God, I come, I come.

Just as I am, and waiting not to rid my soul of one dark blot, to Thee whose blood can cleanse each spot, O Lamb of God, I come, I come.

Just as I am, though tossed about with many a conflict, many a doubt, fightings and fears within, without, O Lamb of God, I come, I come.

Just as I am poor, wretched, blind; sight, riches, healing of the mind, yea all I need in Thee I find, O Lamb of God, I come, I come.

Just as I am, Thou wilt receive, wilt welcome, pardon, cleanse, relieve; because Thy promise I believe, O Lamb of God, I come, I come.

By Charlotte Elliott and William B. Bradbury

Lesson 3 – God's Comfort from His Faithfulness, His Power and Strength -

Psalms of Lament and Expressing Words of Gratitude

Introduction

This lesson looks at how God comforts His children by His faithfulness and through His power and strength. The last part of the lesson focuses on another of David's Psalms of Lament to see how he processes his grief before God and then the challenge to create in you a heart of gratitude before the Lord for His faithfulness and His strength and His power.

Days 1 and 2 – God's Comfort Comes from His Faithfulness as He Is Trustworthy

1.   The comfort God brings to His children a stronger faith in Him in whatever circumstance being faced. Believing in God and the promises in His word will lessen and remove fear, because our God is faithful to His word, and He is trustworthy. Because our God is faithful, we can live by faith and not by fear; whether it be fear of immediate circumstances or fear of the future. Open in **prayer** and then consider these **observation questions**.

➤ <u>What</u> does David say about the LORD in Psalm 145:13?

➤ <u>What</u> is said about the LORD of hosts in Psalm 46:10-11 and <u>what</u> does this ask of us?[14]

➤ <u>What</u> do these verses say about God's faithfulness?

a. Psalm 37:3 (See the footnote for the **word study** for faithfulness in Question 2.)

b. Psalm 25:1[15]

---

[14] To Israel, the phrase LORD of Hosts meant their God is *Yahweh Sabaoth*, the God of a host of angel armies.

[15] In Psalm 25:1 David declares his trust in his God. This is the same Hebrew word "trust" that is in Proverbs 3:5. Read Proverbs 3:5-6 and reflect on the command associated with the Hebrew word "trust" used in both of these verses.

c. Isaiah 43:2

➢ We can believe in God's faithfulness because we believe in His holy word. Look at the context of what became known to Israel as the *Shema* in the opening of Deuteronomy 6. <u>What</u> commands are given in this passage in Deuteronomy 6, and <u>what</u> are the promises made to Israel in Deuteronomy 6:1-9?

➢ <u>How</u> does Moses testify of God's faithfulness in Deuteronomy 32:4?

➢ <u>What</u> did God promise to Joshua in Joshua 1:5-9?

➢ <u>How</u> do these NT passages confirm God's promise to Joshua in Joshua 1:5-9?

a. Matthew 28:18-20

b. Hebrews 13:5-6

➢ <u>What</u> does David declare about himself and about his LORD in Psalm 63:8?

2.   Here are some **word studies** for some **key words** in this lesson.

Strong's # and Transliteration:	Definition from Strong's Concordance, unless written in italics:	Use of the word in other Scriptures:
530 *emuwnah* Psalm 37:3[16]	**Faithfulness**, literally. firmness; figuratively, security; morally, fidelity: faith (-ful, -ly, -ness, [man]), set office, stability, steady, truly, truth, verily	Psalm 36:5
539 *aman* Deuteronomy 7:9	**Faithful**, to build up or support; to foster as a parent or nurse; figuratively, to render (or be) firm or faithful, to trust or believe, to be permanent or quiet; morally, to be true or certain; . . . assurance, believe, bring up, establish, + fail, be faithful (of long continuance, stedfast, sure, surely, trusty, verified), nurse, (-ing father), (put), trust	Jeremiah 42:5
1697 *dabar* Psalm 105:42	**Promise**, see the **word study** for word in Lesson 1.	Psalm 106:12
1862 *epaggelma* 2 Peter 1:4	**Promises**, a self-committal (by assurance of conferring some good); promise. From # 1861, to announce upon, to engage to do something, to assert something resting oneself): profess, (make) promises.	Hebrews 9:15
1860 *epaggelia* 2 Corinthians 1:20	**Promises**, an announcement (for information, assent or pledge; especially, a divine assurance of good): message, promise	1 Corinthians 7:1 (This refers back to what Paul quoted from the OT in 1 Corinthians 7:16-18.)
8551 *tamak* Psalm 63:8	**Upholds**, to sustain, by implication to obtain, keep, fast, figuratively to help, follow close: (take up-) hold, (up), maintain, retain, stay (up)	Isaiah 41:10
982 *batach* Psalm 25:1	**Trust**, to hide for refuge, . . . be confident or sure: be bold (confident, secure, sure), . . . put confidence, (make to) hope, (put, make to) trust	Proverbs 3:5
4103 *pistos* 2 Corinthians 1:18	**Faithful**, trustworthy, trustful: believe (-ing, -r), faithful (-ly), sure, true	Hebrews 10:23
3374 *yirah* Psalm 111:10	**Fear**, morally, reverence: dreadful, exceedingly, fearfulness. The verbal form, #3372: *yare*, to fear, to revere, to frighten, (be, had, in) reverence.	Proverbs 9:10

[16] Psalm 37:3 can be translated as "His faithfulness." God's promise of "the land" was fulfilled by the coming of Christ who brought the kingdom of heaven, (Matthew 4:17) and/or the kingdom of God, (Mark 1:15).

Strong's # and Transliteration:	Definition from Strong's Concordance, unless written in italics:	Use of the word in other Scriptures:
4102 *pistis* Revelation 2:13	**Faith**, persuasion, i.e. moral conviction (of religious truth, or the truthfulness of God or a religious teacher), especially reliance upon Christ for salvation; . . . assurance, belief	Hebrews 11:1

3.   In Hebrews 11, we are presented with a reminder of OT individuals who lived "by faith," as they demonstrated their belief in God and His word. Read the summary statement about Abraham and Sarah in Hebrews 11:8-10 to see how the challenges God brought to them are briefly summarized. The lives of Abraham and Sarah are presented in Genesis 12-25. What do these verses in Genesis say about Abraham and his relationship with the LORD?

a. Genesis 12:1-3

b. Genesis 15:1, 6

c. Genesis 22:1-18

4.   Throughout the Bible, God reveals prophecies and promises for people. These prophecies foretell God's plans for the future and His promises reveal His faithfulness. Many of the OT prophecies concern God's promises, such as the land He promised to Israel, the prophecy of the promised new covenant, and the coming of the promised Messiah. OT scholar Walter Kaiser writes that "the promise-plan of God . . . is indeed His own Word and plan, both in His person and His works, to communicate a blessing to Israel and thereby to bless all the nations of the earth."[17] When a promise is made in Scripture, we can depend on the very nature of God as He is faithful to His word.

---

[17] Walter C. Kaiser, Jr. "Promise," *Holman Bible Dictionary* (Nashville, TN: Holman Bible Publisher, 1991), 1141.

A very important reference to "promises" is given by the Holy Spirit through Peter in the opening of 2 Peter. Read what is said in 2 Peter 1:3-11. How is the word "promise" used in this passage?

Paul made an important declaration in 2 Corinthians 1:20 about God's promises. Look back at this portion of Paul's letter to see his testimony from v. 12 and summarize what he declares about the promises of God, Christ Jesus, and the Holy Spirit in vv. 18-24.

The same word "faithful" that Paul used in 2 Corinthians 1:18 is used in 1 Corinthians 1:9. Write out these important truths and meditate on these declarations.

a. 2 Corinthians 1:18

b. 1 Corinthians 1:9

How did the author of Hebrews use the words "promised" and "faithful" in Hebrews 10:23 and what does this verse ask of those who believe in Jesus? (The word translated as "hold fast" in this verse can also be understood as "keep in memory.")

Think about what causes you to forget what Scripture says about our God and the impact this has had on you in the past. How can you "hold fast . . . without wavering"?

5.　　What is revealed about David's relationship with God in Psalm 143? Imagine singing these words that were inspired by the Holy Spirit. What does David testify about his pattern of living and his commitment to the LORD in vv. 5-8?

6.   Sometimes God's promises to His people contain a "condition" for the promise. The commands of what became known as "The *Shema*" in Deuteronomy 6:4-9 were introduced by a significant promise for Israel in v. 3. This word "promised" in v. 3 is the Hebrew verbal form of the noun "promise" defined in the **word studies** above. The Hebrew *dabar* is the word often translated into English as "word" and to Israel it is associated with the Ten Commandments which were written by God on stone and were considered as "unchanging and eternal." When the Ten Commandments are mentioned in Deuteronomy 4:13, they are referred to as the Ten *Dabarim*, the Ten Words. The Hebrew *dabarim* is the plural form of *dabar*. In the OT books of prophecy, we find the phrase, "the word of the LORD came to . . ."

In the context of the promise in Deuteronomy 6:3, we see the word "then" in v. 12. What does God ask of His people in vv. 4-9 and what attitude does God ask of His people in vv. 12-19?

7.   God's comfort can increase one's faith and help believers trust in Him. In Psalm 40, David testifies of the character and ministry of his God. Psalm 40 is considered a Psalm of Lament. Read this psalm and summarize what David says in Psalm 40:10-12.

What does David ask of God in Psalm 40:13, 15-17?

We need to remember God's promises to help us before the weight of grief, sorrow, and confusion consumes us. We are to trust God's faithfulness and seek Him. When God makes a promise He is faithful to bring the promise to fruition. Think about the Scriptures that have been studied and reflect on your response to the promises made by God and Jesus Christ and what these promises mean to you today. Those who believe in Jesus as Messiah have received the gift of the Holy Spirit who indwells us to help us remember God's faithfulness.

No matter how HARD our circumstances, we must trust in the faithfulness of our God. Is this easy? No, it is often not easy. Read David's words in Psalm 56, noting especially vv. 3, 4, and 11. What does David declare in these verses and why, according to vv. 8-11?

In Joel 2:25 God promised that He would "restore the years that the locusts have eaten." Life has consequences that come from our sin and the sin of others. God restores us through the blood of Christ's sacrifice and the forgiveness of sin. We must learn to trust in God's sovereignty in the midst of the unknown and uncertainty, and to rest in Him. Some Scriptures can cause us to struggle. What is said about God in Deuteronomy 29:29?

Pastor Dietrich Bonhoeffer who stood up against Adolf Hitler was put in jail for his stand and then murdered. Bonhoeffer said of God, "God's with us in the sweet by and by, but also in the bitter here and now." Jim Elliott who was martyred for his faith when he served as a missionary in Equador said, "The only way to learn strong faith is to endure great trials." Our God is faithful. To have faith in God will take away fear: the faithfulness of God brings comfort. This certainly doesn't mean we are not to grieve, but we must choose to "grieve with God," expressing our sorrow and lament before Him. Even when a serious illness is diagnosed, even when Hospice is called, even when the divorce papers are signed, and even when an important dream does not come to fulfillment.

We looked at Proverbs 3:5-6 earlier. What do hese verses say will define our "trust" and what is promised for us?

In the early Christian church, the leaders found Scripture passages where God and Christ were worshiped by assigning glory to them. The Greek word *doxa* is translated as various forms of "glory" and these passages became part of the church expressing "words of glory" to their heavenly Father and their Savior Jesus Christ. These "words of glory" became known as doxologies from the two words in the Greek, *doxa* and *logos*, which is generally translated into "word," "message," or "oracle." The English word doxology was then given as the designation for the two Greek words that focused worship on proclaiming "words" of "glory" to God and Jesus. The verses found in Revelation 1:5-6 became a "doxology" for the early church. As you read these words, reflect again on what is being declared here. I have written the truths proclaimed in these verses in my own words to declare my worship before my Savior Jesus and my Father, God.

In the doxology in Revelation 1:5-6, significant truths are revealed aobut Jesus, among which Jesus is called "the faithful One." "From Jesus, the witness, the faithful One, the first born from the dead, the ruler over the kings of the earth; the One who loves me and has freed me from my sin by His blood and has made me a member of His kingdom, a priest for my God and Father, to You, Jesus, be glory and power forever and ever! Amen," (Revelation 1:5-6).

Not only is Jesus all of these declarations in Revelation 1:5-6, He is also a Friend to those who believe in Him, (John 15:14). The hymn "What a Friend We Have in Jesus" expresses His faithfulness to us. You might sing this as your closing prayer before your faithful God and Father and your faithful Savior Jesus. Jesus also taught that the indwelling Holy Spirit would be with us "forever," (John 14:16).

"What a Friend We Have in Jesus"

What a Friend we have in Jesus, all our sins and griefs to bear! What a privilege to carry everything to God in prayer! O what peace we often forfeit, O what needless pain we bear, all because we do not carry everything to God in prayer!

Have we trials and temptations? Is there trouble anywhere? We should never be discouraged, take it to the Lord in prayer. Can we find a friend so faithful who will all our sorrows share? Jesus knows our every weakness, take it to the Lord in prayer.

Are we weak and heavy laden, cumbered with a load of care? Precious Saviour, still our refuge – take it to the Lord in prayer. Do thy friends despise, forsake thee? Take it to the Lord in prayer; in His arms He'll take and shield thee, thou wilt find a solace there.

By Joseph Scriven and Charles C. Converse

Days 3 and 4 - God's Comfort Comes through His Power and Strength

1.   Psalm 46 opens with the declaration, "God is our refuge and strength, a very present help in trouble, therefore we will not fear, though the earth should change and though the mountains slip into the heart of the sea," (Psalm 46:1-2). The focus of this portion of the lesson is that God comforts us with His power and strength, as God "Almighty" and "the LORD of hosts." Open in **prayer** to seek the Lord's wisdom as you study some Scriptures focusing on these themes. Begin with these **observation questions**.

➢ <u>What</u> does David say about the LORD in Psalm 37:39-40?

➢ What does the psalmist ask of God and what does he say is his own responsibility in Psalm 71:18?

➢ What are the promises made concerning strength and patience in these verses?

a. Isaiah 40:28-31

b. Psalm 25:21

c. Proverbs 20:22

➢ What promises does God make and what does He say to remind us about His nature in Isaiah 41:10-14?

➢ How is God identified in 1 Corinthians 10:13 and what instruction is given in v. 14? (Someone once said that idolatry is putting anyone or anything above God. That idea can bring conviction, especially when we realize we are grieving as one without hope.)

➢ What did Paul ask concerning his "health" and how did the Lord answer him in 2 Corinthians 12:7-10?

➢ Paul shared his personal testimony with the church in Philippi at the end of his letter. What does Paul declare about God and the people of Philippi in Philippians 4:12-14?

2.   Here are some **word studies** for some of the **key words** in this lesson.

Strong's # and Transliteration:	Definition from Strong's Concordance, unless written in italics:	Use of the word in other Scriptures:
1369 *gebuwrah* Psalm 71:18	**Strength**, force (literally or figuratively); by implication, valor, victory: force, mastery, might, mighty (act, power), strength	Psalm 106:8 Jeremiah 10:6
6960 *qavah* Isaiah 40:31	**Wait for**, to bind together with, (as a rope that is twisted together); to expect together, to look patiently, to wait for, on, or upon	Proverbs 20:22
7706 *shaddai* Genesis 17:1	**Almighty**, *(self-) sufficient, most omnipotent, sovereign*[18]	Exodus 6:3
6635 *sabaoth* Psalm 24:10	**Hosts**, a mass of persons (or figuratively things), especially regarding organized for war (an army); by implication a campaign, literally or figuratively (specifically hardship, worship). *The word "had military overtones."*[19]	Joshua 5:14
6937 *qadar* Psalm 43:2	**Mourning**, to be ashy, i.e. dark-colored; by implication, to mourn (in sackcloth or sordid garments): be black (-ish), be (make) dark (-en), heavily, (cause to) mourn	Job 5:11
1411 *dunamis* 2 Corinthians 12:9	**Power**, force (literally or figuratively); specifically, miraculous power (usually by implication, a miracle itself): ability, abundance, meaning, might (-ily, -y, -y deed), (worker of) miracle (-s), strength, violence, mighty (wonderful) work	Ephesians 3:16
1412 *dunamoo* Phil. 4:12	**Strength,** to enable, to strengthen (from #1411)	Ephesians 3:16
4599 *sthenoo* 1 Peter 5:10	**Strengthen**, (bodily vigor), i.e. figuratively, to confirm (in spiritual knowledge and power)	*A hapax legomen.*

[18]BDB. Ibid., 995.

[19]Spiros Zodhiates, "Lexical Aids to the Old Testament," *The Hebrew-Greek Key Study Bible* (Chattanooga, TN: AMG Publishers, 1990), 1767.

3. David uses the phrase "the LORD of hosts" in his response to the army of the Philistines in 1 Samuel 17:45. In this context, David uses the word as the "literal" armies of Israel. The word later became associated with the "host or armies of angels" that God sent to defend His people. In the book of Amos, we read a prophecy of judgment for Israel's enemies as well as a prophecy of judgment to the northern kingdom of Israel. In these prophecies, God reminds Israel of His sovereignty and His power. Read Amos 4:13 to see how the phrase "the LORD God of hosts" is used. At the end of God's prophecy in Amos, this same phrase is used that is in Amos 9:5. Give several examples of how the LORD of hosts is described in the context of these two passages.

4. When the southern kingdom of Judah was threatened by the Moabites, the Ammonites, and the Meunites, King Jehoshaphat gathered the people of Judah together. What was the king's attitude that is recorded in 2 Chronicles 20:3 and what did he do according to vv. 4-5?

Read Jehoshaphat's prayer in 2 Chronicles 20:6-12 to see how he addressed the LORD in his prayer.

I am so blessed when I read the king's response to God in 2 Chronicles 20:12. I am convicted by his faith in God when he faced a difficult situation. How does King Jehoshaphat testify of his faith in the LORD?

5. David declared of his God, "For You have been a refuge for me, a tower of strength against the enemy. Let me dwell in Your tent forever; let me take refuge in the shelter of Your wings," (Psalm 61:3-4). Read what was said of David's great grandmother, Ruth, years before. Ruth was from Moab and she had married a man from Israel who died. As a widow, Ruth went to Israel with her mother-in-law after the famine ended that sent this family out of Israel into

the land of Moab. What does Boaz say about Ruth in Ruth 2:11-12? (Remember that Boaz was the son of Rahab, of Jericho, and Salmon.)

Read what is said about God in Nahum 1:7 and what this asks of those who trust in Him.

In Lesson 1 you studied the armor we have been given by the Lord. As a reminder, write out the instructions in Ephesians 6:10-11,13 and the reason these instructions are given.

In Hannah's Prayer in 1 Samuel 2:1-10, which is called a song of thanksgiving, she testifies of her heart exulting in the LORD and her horn being exalted in Him. The word "horn" was used as a symbol of strength, power, and prosperity. 1 Samuel 1 explains Hannah's heartache and her plea before God for a child. What does Hannah declare in her song, especially in 1 Samuel 2:1, 4 that shows her response to her God?

Here's a challenge! Think back on the passages of Scripture you studied in this portion of the lesson and pick a verse to memorize. The spiritual discipline of Bible memorization will strengthen you and help you stand firm against the struggles that you face today or will face in the future. You could write out your verse here as the first step to memorizing the verse.

Do you remember the hymn "A Mighty Fortress" that Martin Luther wrote in the 16th century? This hymn is a powerful reminder of the nature of our God and His faithfulness and power.

"A Mighty Fortress"

> *A mighty fortress is our God, a bulwark never failing; our helper He amid the flood of mortal ills prevailing. For still our ancient foe doth seek to work us woe, his craft and pow'r are great, and armed with cruel hate, on earth is not his equal.*
>
> *Did we in our own strength confide our striving would be losing, were not the right Man on our side, the Man of God's own choosing. Dost ask who that may be? Christ Jesus, it is He – Lord Sabaoth His name, from age to age the same, and He must win the battle.*
>
> *And though this world, with devils filed, should threaten to undo us, we will not fear, for God hath willed His truth to triumph through us. The prince of darkness grim – we tremble not for him; His rage we can endure, for lo! His doom is sure, one little word shall fell him.*
>
> *That word above all earthly powers – no thanks to them abideth; the Spirit and the gifts are ours through Him who with us sideth. Let goods and kindred go, this mortal life also; the body they may kill; God's truth abideth still, His kingdom is forever. Amen.*
>
> By Martin Luther

Day 5 – A Look at Some Psalms of Lament and Expressing Words of Gratitude

1.   This week you have looked at Scriptures focusing on the faithfulness and power of our Father God, our Savior, Jesus, and the Holy Spirit. Isaiah 25:1 declares "O LORD, You are my God; I will exalt You, I will give thanks to Your name; for You have worked wonders, in plans formed long ago, with perfect faithfulness." Remember studying Psalm 136 and the phrase that was repeated for emphasis to help people remember the nature of their God; "His lovingkindness is everlasting." Open in **prayer** acknowledging God's faithfulness and His power and then begin these **observation questions**.

➢ David's Psalm 41 is considered a Psalm of Lament, with the "lament" in vv. 4-10. <u>What</u> is the "lament" David brings before God in these verses?

➢ <u>What</u> does David ask of God in vv. 4-10?

➢ <u>What</u> does David say about God in vv. 1-3, 11-13?

2.   Here are some **word studies** for some of the **key words** in this lesson.

Strong's # and Transliteration:	Definition from Strong's Concordance, unless written in italics:	Use of the word in other Scriptures:
5315 *nephesh* Psalm 41:4	**Soul**, a breathing creature, i.e. animal or (abstract) vitality, used very widely in a literal accommodated or figurative sense (bodily or mental): . . . soul; *life*	Psalm 103:1-2

Strong's # and Transliteration:	Definition from Strong's Concordance, unless written in italics:	Use of the word in other Scriptures:
8426 *towdah* Psalm 100:4	**Thanksgiving**, see the **word study** for thanksgiving in Lesson 1	Psalm 26:7
8416 *tehillah* Psalm 100:4	**Praise**, see the **word study** for praiseworthy in Lesson 2	Psalm 47:6, 7
3034 *yada* Isaiah 25:1	**Thank**, see the **word study** for thank in Lesson 1	Psalm 92:1
6031 *anah* Psalm 35:13	**Humble**, through the idea of looking down or browbeating]; to depress literally or figuratively . . . (in various applications, as follow): abase self, afflict (-ion, self), . . . chasten self, deal hardly with, defile, . . . humble (self), hurt, ravish, . . . submit self	Leviticus 16:29 (This is the verbal form, #6030.)

3.   OT biblical scholar, Nobuyoshi Kiuchi posits that in many Scriptures, the Hebrew word *nephesh* carries the meaning of "the soul" and he defines the word as the "self-enhancing nature."[20] In Psalm 103:1-2 David said, "Bless the LORD, O my soul, and all that is within me bless His holy name. Bless the LORD, O my soul, and forget none of His benefits." David testified that he humbled his soul with fasting in Psalm 35:13. Dr. Kiuchi says that the human soul can keep people from surrendering to God. I think of the soul as the bent of a toddler, who wants their own way rather than the instruction of those in authority over them. The world is familiar with the song that declares, "I did it my way." What does it say in Judges 17:6; 21:25 about the people of Israel during the time of the Judges?

The most holy day for the nation of Israel is the Day of Atonement, *Yom Kippur*. Read what is required of the people in Leviticus 16:29-31n concerning their response to God.

4.   Psalm 43 is also considered as a Psalm of Lament. Read the psalm and look for what is asked of God and what the psalmist declares about God in this psalm.

My friend Joe has a motto that he puts into action when life is hard. Joe reminds himelf to just keep "putting one foot in front of the other," to keep moving and keep walking in faithful obedience to God's word. Someone said that the word "endurance" can simply be

[20]Nobuyoshi Kiuchi, *Leviticus* (Nottingham, UK: Apollos, 2007), 364.

understood as "to keep walking" or "to keep going " in the midst of what God has put before you.

Think about your own life at the present time. Is there something you are struggling with personally? Pray and ask God to help you write out your own psalm of lament, perhaps modeling your psalm after Psalm 41 or Psalm 43. Your psalm of lament might reflect a struggle you have in which you need to trust in God's faithfulness and not rely on your own strength. Turn to the place in the Appendix to write out your psalm.

When we are grieving, we need to trust in God's faithfulness. When we are grieving, we need to ask God for His strength. In closing, read Psalm 100 to look at how the psalmist acknowledged God and the commands that are given in response to God.

The author of Hebrews challenges believers to "let us continually offer up a sacrifice of praise to God, that is the fruit of lips that give thanks to His name," (Hebrews 13:15). May this truly be the pattern of our days. Turn to the page in the Appendix that asks you to come before the Lord and write down your Psalm of Thanksgiving, including at least five ways that you are grateful to God, expressing your thankfulness before Him.

Close in a prayer of gratitude and praise, seeking God's help and His strength in an area where you desire to be victorious in your own walk with the Lord while looking at this hymn.

"I Surrender All"

All to Jesus I surrender, all to Him I freely give; I will ever love and trust Him, in His presence daily live.

Refrain: I surrender all, I surrender all, all to Thee, my blessed Savior, I surrender all.

All to Jesus I surrender, humbly at His feet I bow; worldly pleasures all forsaken, take me Jesus, take me now.

Refrain:

All to Jesus, I surrender, make me Saviour, wholly Thine; let me feel the Holy Spirit, truly know that Thou art mine.

Refrain:

All to Jesus I surrender, Lord I give myself to Thee; fill me with Thy love and power, let Thy blessing fall on me.

Refrain:

By Judson W. Van de Venter and Winfield S. Weeden

Lesson 4 – God's Comfort Comes from His Wisdom and Peace –

Psalms of Lament and Expressing Words of Gratitude

Introduction

This lesson looks at how God comforts us through His infinite wisdom and His exhortation for believers to be wise. The lesson also studies what it means to have God's peace, which Paul promises "passes all understanding" (Philippians 4:6). What does the Bible mean by the words "wisdom, "wise," and "peace" and how can we find comfort in these truths? I will continue to trust my loving heavenly Father and my Savior Jesus to minister to me in my grief through the faithfulness and ministry of the indwelling Holy Spirit who comforts, helps, and counsels me in every circumstance I face.

Doctors have designated a "new" understanding of a type of grief called "ambivalent grief," designated as the grief associated with caring for a loved one who is suffering from dementia, Alzheimer's, or traumatic brain injury. In this grief, there's no knowing how the condition will "unfold" or the timing of what is ahead. For those who believe in Jesus, during this "ambivalent grief," God's wisdom and His peace minister in a very significant way.

Days 1 and 2 – God's Comfort Comes from His Wisdom

1.   A change of one's circumstances can lead to grief. Sometimes a loss or grievous situation can bring confusion about how to face the unknown influences of the future. When we are in "new" circumstances, we can always turn to our God for His wisdom. Open your time in the word in **prayer** and then begin with these **observation questions**.

➤ Read the opening of the book of Proverbs to see <u>what</u> is said about the words "wise" and "wisdom" in Proverbs 1:2-7.

➤ Many believers have memorized Proverbs 3:5-6 and verses 7 and 8 that follow relate to another way our God comforts us. We are given specific instructions in this passage, as well as exhortations and promises. As you read these verses, underline the instructions and draw a circle around those phrases that encourage you.

"Trust in the LORD with all your heart, and lean not on your own understanding. In all your ways acknowledge Him, and He will make your paths straight. Do not be wise in your own eyes; fear the LORD and turn away from evil. It will be healing to your body, and refreshment to your bones," (Proverbs 3:5-8).

➤ The word "healing" in v. 8 carries a meaning that involves a process of restoration, given in the context for someone who lives in "the fear of the LORD." Think back on the opening of Proverbs to see how Proverbs 3:5-8 relates to the introduction in Proverbs 1:2-7. <u>How</u> do these passages challenge you personally?

➤ Read Psalm 51 and reflect on <u>what</u> David asks of God in Psalm 51:1-6.

➤ <u>What</u> does David say about himself in Psalm 51:1-6?

➤ <u>What</u> does David declare about God in Psalm 51:6?

➤ The word "wisdom" is used in Colossians 3:16-17. Look at <u>how</u> instructions are given in these verses for the individual and <u>what</u> that is to mean to other believers.

2.   Here are some **word studies** for some **key words** in this lesson.

Strong's # and Transliteration:	Definition from Strong's Concordance, unless written in italics:	Use of the word in other Scriptures:
2451 *chokmah* Proverbs 1: 2, 7; 8:1	**Wisdom**, (in a good sense): skillful, wisely, wit. In the OT, the word is most often used as "*wisdom, prudence in religious affairs.*"[21]	Deuteronomy 4:6
2450 *chakawm* Proverbs 3:7	**Wise**, intelligent, skillful, or artful: cunning of man, and unwise, wise (hearted, man)	Psalm 107:43
2449 *chakam* Psalm 119:98	**Insight**, to be wise, (in mind, word, or act): exceeding, teach wisdom, be (make self, show self), deal wisely, make wiser	Proverbs 9:9 (Look at Proverbs 9:10 to see the word #2451.)

---

[21] BDB, Ibid., 315.

Strong's # and Transliteration:	Definition from Strong's Concordance, unless written in italics:	Use of the word in other Scriptures:
4678 *sophia* James 1:5	**Wisdom**, (higher or lower, worldly or spiritual). *"Transcendent wisdom that God imparts to those who are close to God"*[22]	James 3:17
4680 *sophos* Romans 16:19	**Wise**, (in a most general application.[23] *In the NT "wise in that the wisdom is divine in nature and origin. . . . pertaining to understanding that results in wise attitudes and conduc*t."[24]	Ephesians 5:15 1 Corinthians 1:26
3374 *yirah* Psalm 111:10	**Fear**, see the **word study** for fear in Lesson 3	Proverbs 9:10

3.   In the book of Deuteronomy, God is preparing His people to enter the land He promised to them. What did God command of His people and why in Deuteronomy 4:6? (You must look back at the verses that come before to see what is meant by the word "them" in this verse.)

The Bible records one psalm attributed to Moses. According to Psalm 90:12, what does Moses ask of God? (Psalm 90 is also studied later as a Psalm of Lament.)

Because Psalm 90:12 opens with the word "so" we need to look at the verse in the context of the psalm. What does Moses declare about God in his psalm that leads him to his comments in verse 12?

4.   Solomon followed his father David as king over Israel. Read the opening of 1 Kings 3 and then summarize what Solomon asked of God in his prayer that is recorded in 1 Kings 3:6-9.

---

[22] BDAG, Ibid., 934.

[23] James Strong compares the Greek word *phronimos* (#5429) with *sophos* (#4680). *Phronimos* carries the meaning of "thoughtful, i.e. sagacious or discreet (implying a cautious character); while #4680 denotes practical skill or acumen." Ibid., 66.

[24] BDAG, Ibid., 935.

How did God answer Solomon according to 1 Kings 3:10-14?

As we studied in Lesson 1, in the new covenant that was brought by the blood of Jesus, the Holy Spirit indwells believers so that we have a helper, comforter, and counselor who guides us into God's truth to teach us "all things," (John 14:16, 26). Think about how this compares with what God said to Solomon to give him "a wise and discerning heart, so that there has been no one like you before you nor shall one like you arise after you," (1 Kings 3:13).

Think about God's gift of wisdom that is possible through the ministry of the Holy Spirit and write out what is said about God in James 1:5-6.

Later in James 3, James presents a powerful contrast between the wisdom "from the world" and the wisdom "from above." James would have used the phrase "from above" out of reverence for God as the people of Israel did after returning from Persian captivity. In reverence to God, the people of Israel would not "verbalize" the name of God. Another example of this is in the NT when Matthew's gospel uses the phrase "kingdom of heaven" rather than the "kingdom of God."

Write out the qualities of God's wisdom and then what James says about the wisdom that does not comes from above in James 3:13-15 to see how some of these qualities would be considered the "opposite" of the "wisdom from above."

The Wisdom from Above: James 3:17-18	The Wisdom from the World: James 3:13-16

How can these characteristics of God's wisdom bring you comfort?

5.   The psalmist wrote in Psalm 111:10, "The fear of the LORD is the beginning of wisdom; all who follow His instructions have good insight, His praise endures forever." This verse has a strong connection with Proverbs 1:7, "The fear of the LORD is the beginning of knowledge; fools despise wisdom and instruction." Remember in Lesson 2 where Bruce Waltke's definition of the phrase "the fear of the LORD" is shared. Dr. Waltke defined the phrase as a response to the Lord so that someone falls on their knees and waves a white flag of surrender. How does the teaching in Psalm 111:10 and Proverbs 1:7 help you understand Dr. Waltke's definition?

OT biblical scholar, Artur Weiser quotes Paul Gerhardt's comments on David's Psalm 37 and calls David's Psalm of Lament a "song of confidence" commanding us to "'commit thou all thy griefs,'"[25] unto the LORD in whom David says we are to rest and wait patiently for Him, (Psalm 37:7). The word wisdom is mentioned in Psalm 37:30. Read Psalm 37 and look for truths that David declared about God. List ten truths about God from this Psalm and reflect on what these qualities of God mean to you today.

The Holy Spirit led David to write commands in Psalm 37. What are five commands included in David's Psalm of Lament?

---

[25] Artur Weiser, *The Psalms*, translated by Herbert Hartwell (Philadelphia, PA: Westminster Press, 1962), 314.

Can you claim these truths as David did? What gets in the way of you knowing and trusting God as David did?

God's wisdom also shows us how to have compassion for others who are grieving. In the Hebrew language, words have male, female, or neuter gender. The Hebrew word for wisdom is in the feminine, so when Proverbs 8 presents teaching about wisdom, it is referred to as "she." Read Proverbs 8 to see what Israel understood about wisdom and meditate on this teaching and close in a prayer before the Lord.

Days 3 and 4 – God's Comfort Comes from His Peace

1.   This portion of the lesson focuses on how we can have peace in the midst of our grief because of the faithfulness of our Lord God, our Savior Jesus, and the Holy Spirit. Isaiah 54:10, says, "'For the mountains may depart and the hills be removed, but my steadfast love shall not depart from you, and my covenant of peace shall not be removed,' says the Lord, who has compassion on you." Jesus was prophesied as the "Prince of peace" in Isaiah 9:6 and Jesus promised that He would leave His peace when He ascended to heaven. Jesus described this peace as a peace that is not of this world, and then commanded His followers to "Let not your heart be troubled, nor let it be afraid," (John 14:27). Open in **prayer** and begin with these **observation questions**.

> ➤ Write out the message God gave to Moses for Aaron and his sons to speak to the sons of Israel, in Numbers 6:24-26. (These verses became known as the Aaronic Benediction.) These are really GOOD verses to memorize!

> ➤ <u>What</u> did God ask of Aaron and his sons in Numbers 6:27 and <u>what</u> is the promise that follows?

> ➤ <u>What</u> command does David voice in Psalm 34:14?

➤ Hebrews 12:14 quotes a portion of Psalm 34:14. <u>What</u> does the author of Hebrews associate with David's psalm in Hebrews 12:14?

➤ <u>What</u> does Paul say about our salvation in these verses?

    a. Romans 5:1-2

    b. Colossians 3:15

➤ Sometimes our grief comes from a broken relationship. <u>What</u> is said in Romans 12:18 about this circumstance and based on truths you know from Scripture, <u>what</u> could help in this kind of situation?

2.   Here are some **word studies** for some of the **key words** in this lesson.

Strong's # and Transliteration:	Definition from Strong's Concordance, unless written in italics:	Use of the word in other Scriptures:
7965 *shalom* Isaiah 26:3	**Peace**, safe, i.e. (figuratively) well, happy, friendly; also (abstractly) welfare, i.e. health, prosperity: . . . (good) health, (perfect, such as be at) peace (-able, -ably), prosper (-ity, -ous), rest, safe (-ty), salute, welfare, (all is, be) well, wholly	Isaiah 9:6 Jeremiah 29:11
1515 *eirene* John 14:27	**Peace**, (literally or figuratively); by implication, prosperity: one, quietness, rest, + set at one again	John 16:33

3.   Write out Isaiah 26:3-4 to see what is said about God and what He promises us.

The Holy Spirit's message to us involves the Hebrew word *shalom* being repeated for emphasis, although it is usually translated as "perfect peace" and not "peace, peace."

I think there is a connection between Isaiah 26:3-4 and Philippians 4:6-9. What did Paul challenge believers to do when we are anxious?

What is promised to believers in Philippians 4:6-7?

Following Paul's teaching in Philippians 4:6-7, what are believers commanded to do in Philippians 4:8-9?

This is another powerful passage to memorize; learning its commands so as to lean on its promises.

4.   Jeremiah 29:11 is a well-known verse where the Hebrew word *shalom* is generally translated as "welfare." We need to look at the context of this verse beginning with Jeremiah 29:7 through Jeremiah 29:14a. What did God ask of His people concerning His *shalom*?

What does God promise to His people in this passage?

5.   Psalm 4 is considered a Psalm of Lament. David asks questions of God, reveals truths about God, and testifies of his faith in God. Read Psalm 4 and write out the ways that David's knowledge of God impacted his faith.

Psalm 4:5 offers a simple command to "trust in the LORD." Years ago I learned the significance of what obedience to this command brings. In the midst of struggle, I sometimes simply say, "I trust You, Lord." Elisabeth Elliot, who understood grief, shared, "In every experience of life, the Lord is standing at the door and knocking and saying, 'Will you trust Me in this?'"

Before the people of Israel entered the Promised Land, God reminded them of two important promises in Deuteronomy 28. When Israel was obedient they would be blessed by God and when they were disobedient, they would know God's curses. Many biblical scholars believe these promises from God are still valid today. When I voice the simple words, "I trust You, God, even in my disappointment, frustration, loss, and grief," this declaration contributes to my spirit moving toward the peace of God that passes all understanding. This is what is promised to believers in Philippians 4:7, which follows the commands to pray, make supplication and requests when we are anxious, in Philippians 4:6. Paul promises that God guards our heart and our mind in Christ Jesus in v. 7. Stop and think about what is "robbing" you of your peace today and bring this concern before the Lord.

What does David declare in Psalm 4:8 about peace?

The NT contains several "benedictions" that are often used in today's churches. The book of Hebrews ends with this benediction, "Now the God of peace, who brought up from the dead the great Shepherd of the sheep through the blood of the eternal covenant, even Jesus our Lord, equip you in every good thing to do His will, working in us that which is pleasing in His sight, through Jesus Christ, to whom be glory forever and ever. Amen," (Hebrews 13:20-21).

The testimony of Horatio Spafford reveals his faith in God as the song "It Is Well with My Soul" was written after a series of losses. In 1871 his son died, he lost considerable property in the Chicago fire, and then in 1873 his four daughters died on a ship. Notice the first phrase Mr. Spafford declared in his song.

"It is Well with My Soul"

*When peace, like a river, attendeth my way, when sorrows like sea billows roll –
Whatever my lot, Thou hast taught me to say, it is well, it is well with my soul.*

Chorus: It is well, (it is well), with my soul, (with my soul), it is well, it is well with my soul.

Tho Satan should buffet, tho trials should come, let this blest assurance control, that Christ hath regarded my helpless estate and hath shed His own blood for my soul.

Chorus:

And Lord, haste the day when my faith shall be sight, the clouds be rolled back as a scroll: The trump shall resound and the Lord shall descend, "Even so" – it is well with my soul.

Chorus:

By Horatio Spafford and Philip P. Bliss

Remember Lesson 2 included the prompt to pray through Scripture using the three R's: REJOICE, REPENT, and REQUEST? Choose a passage from this part of the lesson and pray through some of the qualities of God and REJOICE over those that you accept as truth, REPENT over those you struggle with, and REQUEST God's help with changing you, removing what gets in the way of you trusting in your God and Savior. Continue to ask the Holy Spirit to guide you into the truths in God's word, continue to ask the Holy Spirit to comfort you, to help you, and to encourage you. Remember the father who testified before Jesus in Mark 9:17-29 of his belief and his unbelief, saying to Jesus, "I do believe! Help my unbelief," (Mark 9:24). Close in prayer confessing your belief, asking God to help you in those areas where you struggle to believe.

Day 5 – A Look at the Psalms of Lament and Expressing Words of Gratitude

1.   This lesson looked at what God's wisdom means to us as believers and how the Lord brings us peace. As you start this portion of the lesson think back to some of the verses you studied in Lesson 4 and I challenge you to memorize a verse about God's wisdom and/or God's peace from the Scriptures you studied. Trusting God and believing in His word will always bring His wisdom and His peace. Psalm 119:11 testifies of the power of God's word, "Thy word have I hid in my heart that I might not sin against Thee." While this is true, hiding God's word in our heart can also provide a means of ministering to another person. Remember the second part of the verse this study focuses on, "Blessed be the God and Father of our Lord Jesus Christ, the Father of mercies and God of all comfort; who comforts us in all our affliction so that we may be able to comfort those who are in any affliction with the comfort with which we ourselves are comforted by God," (2 Corinthians 1:3-4).

Psalm 90 is considered a Psalm of Lament written by Moses in which he uses the word "wisdom" in v. 12. The **observation questions** focus on Moses' psalm. Open in **prayer** as you begin.

➤   What references to "time" does Moses mention in Psalm 90:1-2?

➤   Moses continues mentioning "time" in vv. 4-6. How does God's concept of "time" differ from ours?

> ➤ How does the teaching in Psalm 90:8 relate to what is said in Hebrews 4:13?

> ➤ What does Moses ask of God in v. 12 and what does he believe will happen when this is fulfilled? (This is written as what is called a purpose clause, as identified through the word "that" or the words "so that.")

> ➤ What does Moses ask of God for himself and others in vv. 13-17?

2.   Here are **word studies** for some **key words** in this part of the lesson.

Strong's # and Transliteration:	Definition from Strong's Concordance, unless written in italics:	Use of the word in other Scriptures:
5278 *noam* Psalm 90:17	**Favor**, pleasantness, beauty	Proverbs 3:17
3559 *kun* Psalm 90:17	**Establish**, to set up, make firm, to prepare, fixed, steadfast; *confirm*	Psalm 8:3

3.   Daniel 10 is a very important account of Daniel's life during the reign of Cyrus, the ruler of the Persian Empire. Begin by reading one verse in the chapter, Daniel 10:19, to see what God did to minister to Daniel.

Now read from the beginning of the chapter to see the circumstances of Daniel's life from v. 2 and following. How was Daniel described in v. 2?

What was the message given to Daniel according to vv. 11-12?

What was Daniel's response to his "visitor" according to vv. 15-18?

God's messenger told Daniel about what was to come in Daniel 11 and 12 through very specific prophecies. In thinking about Daniel 10, what do you learn about God and His means of being the "God of all comfort?"

This passage in Daniel caused me to reflect on Jesus' promises to His followers about the coming of the Holy Spirit who would be our helper, our counselor, and our source of comfort, (John 14:15, 26). I thought about the gift of the Holy Spirit and His ministry to us. Paul also teaches about another dimension of the ministry of the Holy Spirit in Romans 8:26-27. Read these verses in the context of Paul's teaching, beginning with Romans 8:18 through v. 30. Can you see a connection between Daniel 10 and this passage in Romans 8? What does this reveal about God and His provisio Philippians n for you?

The declaration in Daniel 10:19 about Daniel being "treasured" by God reminded me of what Paul said in his opening of Ephesians 1. What is said about those who believe in Ephesians 1:1-14 and meditate on what these truths mean to you today.

4.   You have read several psalms designated as Psalms of Lament and have seen the psalmists cry out to God. Take some time to write out your own psalm of lament concerning the circumstances of your life at this very moment. Often our struggles are focused on circumstances that do not affect us in the immediate future, but more so at a later date. Sometimes we do not understand why God has allowed His children to suffer. We <u>must</u> cry out to God and trust His wisdom. We <u>must</u> turn to God and claim the promises of His peace. Turn to the Appendix and write out your psalm.

We looked at Philippians 4:6-7 earlier and the word "thanksgiving" is used in v. 6. Read again how the word "thanksgiving" is used in this passage and what this means to you today.

Think about the many ways in which you are grateful today, and in your Psalm of Thanksgiving write out five expressions of your gratitude.

As a child, I grew up in a church that sang hymns in the worship service. The hymn "Immortal, Invisible, God Only Wise" was written by a pastor from Scotland who used the music of a Welsh ballad. If you know this melody, sing this as an act of worship or read the words in closing as your personal prayer as the hymn is directed toward God.

"Immortal, Invisible, God Only Wise"

Immortal, invisible, God only wise, in light inaccessible hid from our eyes, most blessed, most glorious, the Ancient of Days, Almighty, victorious, Thy great name we praise.

Unresting, unhasting, and silent as light, nor wanting, nor wasting, Thou rulest in might; Thy justice, like mountains, high soaring above Thy clouds, which are fountains of goodness and love.

To all, life Thou givest to both great and small, in all life Thou livest, the true life of all; we blossom and flourish as leaves on the tree, and wither and perish, but naught changeth Thee.

Great Father of glory, pure Father of light, Thou angels adore Thee, all veiling their sight; all praise we would render, O help us to see 'tis only the splendor of light hideth Thee!

By Walter Chalmers Smith

Lesson 5 – Comfort Comes from Jesus, the Living Hope Who Brings Us Joy -

A Final Look at the Psalms of Lament and Expressing Words of Gratitude

Introduction

This last lesson studies Scripture that declares the hope and joy believers can have when they trust in God's holy word, as the Bible reveals truths about how it is possible to have hope and joy in the midst of difficulties. It can help to understand the opposite of a word to fully comprehend the meaning of a word. Various individuals have offered the following words as those which have a meaning opposite to the word "hope": despair, fear, defeat, pessimism, distrust, and misery. This is quite a list and represents feelings everyone has probably experienced at one time or another. The dictionary lists the antonyms for "joy" as: misery, despair, trial, tribulation, calamity, and ill-being. Did you notice that the words misery and despair appear on both lists? I think having an attitude of hope and joy is to be a goal for believers. It is not just an emotional goal, because hope and joy are deeply rooted in our spiritual well-being and reflect our belief in God. We must choose to believe in His word, or we will never find hope and joy. As we conclude this study on how God comforts us, we explore the meanings behind our hope and how it is possible to have joy.

The hymn, "I Need Thee Every Hour" has always been a favorite of mine. In the third verse the authors confess they need Jesus "every hour, in joy or pain." You might sing or read these words as you open this lesson, in an act of worship before your Savior.

"I Need Thee Every Hour"

I need Thee every hour, most gracious Lord; no tender voice like Thine can peace afford.

Refrain: I need Thee, O I need Thee; every hour I need Thee; O bless me now, my Saviour, I come to Thee!

I need Thee every hour, stay Thou nearby; temptations lose their power when Thou art nigh.

Refrain:

I need Thee every hour, in joy or pain; come quickly and abide, or life is vain.

Refrain:

I need Thee every hour, most Holy One; O make me Thine indeed, Thou blessed Son!

Refrain:

By Annie S. Hawks and Robert Lowry

Days 1 and 2 – God's Comfort Leads to Hope for Christ's Followers

1.   In looking for truths that declare our hope in God and our hope in Jesus, we see that hope has a strong connection with the concept of trust. I think hope can only follow trust, because when we trust in God and have faith in the truths in His word, we can have hope. In Jeremiah

17:7 God says, "Blessed is the man who trusts in the LORD, whose confidence indeed is the LORD." David testifies in Psalm 62:5-8. "My soul, wait in silence for God only, for my hope is from Him. He only is my rock and my salvation, my stronghold; I shall not be shaken. On God my salvation and my glory rest; the rock of my strength, my refuge is in God. Trust in Him at all times, O people; pour out your heart before Him; God is a refuge for us. Selah," (NASB). After Corrie ten Boom was released from Ravensbruck Concentration Camp she said of God, "I've experienced His presence in the deepest darkest hell that men can create. . . I have tested the promises of the Bible, and believe me, you can count on them."

With every grief, a measure of hope can eventually return which helps those who grieve accept their situation. It has been said to parents who have lost a child, "You never get over it, but you must learn to accept" the loss, as painful as that is. Rick Warren testifies after the death of his son, "ministry flows from deep pain."

This portion of the lesson looks at OT passages that testify of individuals who lived in difficult situations, but eventually had "hope" in God, as well as NT passages that declare the hope we have because of Jesus, who is our "living hope," (1 Peter 1:3). Open in **prayer** and begin with these **observation questions**.

➤ Psalm 71:5 declares, "For You are my hope; O Lord (*Adonai*) God (*Yahweh*). *Yahweh* means "the Self-Existent One" and the "Great I AM" as God introduced Himself to Moses in Exodus 3:14.) Who follows this testimony at the end of vv. 5, 7, and in v. 14?

   a. Psalm 71:5b

   b. Psalm 71:7b

   c. Psalm 71:14

➤ Psalm 33 testifies of God's faithfulness and His lovingkindness toward His people. What does Psalm 33:18-22 declare about God?

➤ What does Psalm 33:18-22 ask of believers?

➤ Jeremiah wrote a lament before God that is recorded in the book of Lamentations. In the midst of his suffering and his lament on behalf of his people, Jeremiah declared words of exhortation concerning our God and how he had chosen to respond to Him. The book of Jeremiah records Jeremiah's first direct encounter with God. (Read the opening of Jeremiah to see what God said to Jeremiah and how Jeremiah responded in Jeremiah 1:4-10.)[26]

➤ The truths in Lamentations 3:23 became the focus of several worship songs for the Christian church. Read Lamentations 3:19-32 and write out what is testified of our God in this passage.

➤ What is Jeremiah's personal testimony in Lamentations 3:24 and why does he say this, according to vv. 22-23?

➤ The NT has important teaching about the concept of "hope." Christian hope is bold, involving the choice "to wait for God." What did Peter say about our God and Jesus in 1 Peter 1:3-5?

➤ What did Paul write about Scripture in Romans 15:4-6?

_____

[26] This can bring reflection as to our identity as a believer in Jesus. Read Ephesians 1:3-6 to be reminded of what it means to have an inheritance from God and how this relates to God's words to Jeremiah.

➢ Look back at Romans 15:1-3 to see Paul's concern for the church, especially for how Paul uses the word "edification" in v. 2.

➢ What did Paul announce in Romans 15:13 and how is this claim possible?

➢ In the Epistle to the Hebrews, what is said about Jesus in Hebrews 6:19?

➢ How is the word "faith" defined in Hebrews 11:1? This in fact is the definition of the word "faith" that was used in the first Webster's Dictionary, composed in America in 1831; Webster's definition of faith was simply a quotation of Hebrews 11:1.

2.   Here are some **word studies** for **key words** in this lesson.

Strong's # and Transliteration:	Definition from Strong's Concordance, unless written in italics:	Use of the word in other Scriptures:
8615 *tiqvah* Psalm 71:5	**Hope,** a cord (as an attachment), figuratively, expectance: expectation, . . . *the* thing that I long for	Ruth 1:12 Lamentations 3:29 Jeremiah 29:11; 31:17
113 *Adonai* Psalm 71:5	**Lord,** the Lord (used as a proper name of God only): (my) Lord; an emphatic form of #113 *Adown* (which means) sovereign, i.e. controller (human or divine): lord, master, owner	Psalm 110:1
4009 *mibtach* Psalm 71:5	**Confidence,** a refuge, security or assurance, confidence, hope, sure, trust	Job 8:14; 18:14; 31:24 Psalm 65:6
3176 *yachal* Psalm 71:14	**Hope,** to wait, by implication, (cause to have, make to) hope, be pained, stay, tarry, wait	Lamentations 3:21, 24

Strong's # and Transliteration:	Definition from Strong's Concordance, unless written in italics:	Use of the word in other Scriptures:
2342 *chiyl* Lamentations 3:26	**Hope**, twist or whirl (in a circular or spiral manner), i.e. (specifically) to dance, to writhe in pain . . . or fear, figuratively, to wait, . . . bear	This word forms the root of the word # 3175 used in Lamentations 3:26, closely related to # 3176, see above.
3175 *yachiyl* Lamentations 3:26	**Wait**, expectant: should hope; from # 3176, and its root # 2342 see above	A *hapax legomen.*
7356 *raham* Lamentations 3:22	**Mercy**, see the **word study** for mercy in Lesson 1, Days 1 and 2	Isaiah 63:7 (Of God) Zech. 7:9 (Toward others)
1680 *elpis* 1 Peter 1:3, 21; 3:15	**Hope**, (to anticipate, usually with pleasure); expectation (abstract or concrete) or confidence: faith	2 Corinthians 1:7 Romans 12:12
1679 *elpizo* Hebrews 11:1	**Hoped**, to expect or confide, (have, thing), hoped, (for), trust	1 Peter 1:13 1 Corinthians 13:7
3619 *oikodome* Romans 15:2	**Edification**, architecture, i.e. (concretely) a structure; figuratively, confirmation: building, edify (-ication, -ing)	Romans 14:19
3874 *parakletos* Romans 15:4	**Encouragement**, see the **word study** for comfort in Lesson 1	John 14:16, 26; 15:26; 16:7

3.　　In the book of Job, we learn of a man's suffering and his struggle with the difficult circumstances of his life. Many biblical scholars believed that Job lived during the time of Abraham, or up until the time called "the time of the Patriarchs" of Isaac and the twelve sons of Jacob, who formed the twelve tribes of Israel.

What was Job's response to the first calamity that came to him according to Job 1:21-22?

As Job's suffering continues, how did he respond according to Job 2:10?

What did Job declare in these passages?

a. Job 10:12

b. Job 12:12-13

c. Job 13:15-18

What do you learn about Job's faith in God in these verses?

Read Job 41:33 through Job 42 to see Job's final (recorded) response to God, how God admonished Job's friends, and what the last portion of the book reveals about Job's character in Job 42:10.

What does the ending of Job teach us about being a friend to someone who is grieving?

4.   In Lesson 2 we looked the story about Jacob's son, Joseph was sold into slavery by his brothers and he was taken to Egypt where he eventually was imprisoned. God turned the circumstances around and the Egyptian Pharaoh "set" Joseph "over all the land of Egypt," (Genesis 41:43). Joseph professed his faith in his God to his brothers at the end of Genesis 50 when he said, "'You planned evil against me; God planned it for good to bring about the present result – the survival of many people. Therefore don't be afraid. I will take care of you and your little ones.' And he comforted them and spoke kindly to them," (Genesis 50:20-21, CSB).

Read what is declared about God and those who love Him in Romans 8:28. How does Paul's teaching in Romans 8:28 agree and confirm what Joseph said in Genesis 50?

The truths (from Romans 8:28 and Genesis 50:20) represent significant teaching about God, but sometimes these truths represent truths that are difficult to rest upon when one is in the midst of loss and heartache. Remember in 2 Corinthians 1:3-4 believers are to know that God is the God of all comfort who comforts us in all our affliction so that we may be able to comfort those who are in any affliction with the comfort with which we ourselves are comforted by God. The Holy Spirit ministers to help, comfort, and counsel believers and in this we can turn to the Holy Spirit and seek the help we need for ourselves and for others when we have a connection with someone who is grieving and needs comfort. What do we say to a person who is grieving?

Keep in mind, believers are considered to be "priests," (1 Peter 2:9; Revelation 1:6; 5:10) and one of the roles of the OT priests who represented God to the people was to intercede for the people. We can also claim Peter's message that we are always to be ready to share the hope that is within us, (1 Peter 3:15) with others. Stop and think about what you might share with someone who needs to know the comfort you have received in a time when you were comforted by God.

5. In the book of Ruth, Naomi used the word "hope" in a different way than in the other OT verses we have just read. Read Naomi's response to her two daughters-in-law in Ruth 1:12. (Notice that the word translated as "hope" in this verse is the first word in the **word study** in Question 2.) Naomi had lost her husband and her two sons, but she returned with her daughter in law, Ruth, to her home in Bethlehem after the drought/famine was ended. In Lesson 2 you looked at the genealogy at the end of the book of Ruth which reveals God's faithfulness and His provision.

Dr. Lesley Alderman writes of "Hope Fatigue – an optimism deficiency about the things we cannot control." As a secular author, Alderman offers four means to help individuals cope when one feels "hopeless."

1.) If you feel anxious, practice deep breathing, to inhale slowly and deeply and then exhale slowly, and repeat this several times.

2.) Take care of yourself physically, regarding what you eat, getting adequate sleep, and exercise.

3.) Remind yourself of what is working well in your life: relationships/friendships, children, and job.

4.) Take action about something that is important to you. Maybe join with those in your church to "do" something positive.

Alderman suggests that you think and plan concerning what you <u>can</u> do rather than what you <u>cannot</u>. For those who believe in the Bible, we know while we cannot be "in control," our loving heavenly Father <u>is</u> "in control" of all things. "While it looks like things are out of control, behind the scenes there is a God who has not surrendered His authority," A. W. Tozer.

Steven Curtis Chapman's song, "Don't Lose Heart" offers reminders of what we are to do when we are struggling. The chorus of his song says, "Don't lose heart, don't lose your faith, and don't let go."

Read David's Psalm 31 and notice what David asked in vv. 23-24. How does David describe God in these verses?

Israel understood their God to be a "rock." David opens Psalm 18 saying "I love You LORD, my strength. The LORD is my rock, my fortress, and my deliverer, my God, my mountain where I seek refuge, my shield and the horn of my salvation," (Psalm 18:1-2, CSB). Hannah prayed, "There is no one holy like the LORD. There is no one besides You! And there is no rock like our God," (1 Samuel 2:2, CSB).

Peter quoted several OT passages as prophetic messages of Jesus. What did Peter write in 1 Peter 2:6-8 about Jesus and what does this mean to you?

What does Peter then say about those who believe in Jesus in 1 Peter 2:9-10 and how important is this in describing your identity as a follower of Jesus?

Close by singing, or reading the lyrics to the song, "The Solid Rock" to see the message proclaimed about Jesus, the solid rock and allow these words that open the song to minister to your spirit.

"The Solid Rock"

My hope is built on nothing less than Jesus' blood and righteousness; I dare not trust the sweetest frame, but wholly lean on Jesus' name.

Refrain: On Christ the solid Rock I stand – All other ground is sinking sand, all other ground is sinking sand.

When darkness veils His lovely face, I rest on His unchanging grace; in every high and stormy gale, my anchor holds within the veil.

Refrain:

His oath, His covenant, His blood, support me in the whelming flood; dressed in His righteousness alone, faultless to stand before the throne.

Refrain:

When He shall come with trumpet sound, Oh, may I then in Him be found; dressed in His righteousness alone, faultless to stand before the throne.

Refrain:

By Edward Mote and William B. Bradbury

Days 3 and 4 – God's Comfort Comes from the Joy We Have Because of Our Relationship with Him

1.   James 1:2-3 says we are to consider it all joy when we encounter various trials; knowing that the testing of our faith produces endurance. Then v. 4 adds that endurance must do its perfect and complete work, so that we may be mature and complete, lacking nothing. In considering this teaching, the opening of this passage is difficult to initially accept, which is why it is the last quality being studied, and not at the beginning of the "list." Both the OT and NT share teaching on the significance of "having joy." Open in **prayer** and then look at the **observation questions** focusing on several of the Psalms that include teaching on rejoicing and having joy.

➤   Psalm 42 is considered to be a Psalm of Lament, which has been thought to have been written at the time of Israel's exile. <u>What</u> does the psalmist say about his soul in these verses?
a. Psalm 42:1-2

b. Psalm 42:5-6

c. Psalm 42:11

➤ Psalm 100 is considered to be a Psalm of Thanksgiving. Read the psalm and note <u>what</u> is said in v. 5 about the LORD.

<u>What</u> are the commands in Psalm 100 that relate to our attitude?

➤ <u>What</u> is David's commitment to the LORD according to Psalm 34:1-4?

<u>What</u> does David say we are "to do" in Psalm 34:8-9?

<u>What</u> does David declare about God in Psalm 34:17-19, 22?

➤ <u>What</u> instructions are presented in Psalm 37:3-7, 34?

<u>What</u> are we promised in Psalm 37:23?

➢ <u>What</u> did David say that God had done for him in Psalm 30:11?

➢ David testifies of "how" God turned his mourning into joy in Psalm 30:1, 2, 3, and 5. <u>What</u> does David say in these verses about <u>what</u> God had done for him?

➢ <u>What</u> does David say in Psalm 16:9, 11 about his attitude?

Notice Psalm 16:9 opens with the word "therefore," which calls us to look back at the verse or verses that came before, to see why the text makes a form of conclusion introduced with the word "therefore." Psalm 16 opens with David's prayer and then he testifies of God's provision for him. <u>What</u> is revealed in Psalm 16:7-8 about David's commitment to the LORD?

2.   Here are **word studies** for some **key words** in this part of the lesson.

Strong's # and Transliteration:	Definition from Strong's Concordance, unless written in italics:	Use of the word in other Scriptures:
7442 *ranan* Psalm 5:11	**Sing for joy**, shout aloud for joy, cry out, be joyful, (greatly, make to) rejoice, (cause to) shout (for joy), (cause to), sing (aloud for joy), triumph	Psalm 132:9, 16
8055 *samach* Psalm 5:11	**Rejoice**, to brighten up, i.e. (figuratively,) be (causatively, make) blithe or gleesome: cheer up, be (make) glad, (have, make) joy (-ful), be (make) merry, (cause to, make to) rejoice	Psalm 33:20
2304 *hedwah* Nehemiah 8:10	**Joy**, a feminine noun denoting joy, gladness; the dwelling place of the Lord is the place of joy and gladness	1 Chronicles 16:27
835 *esher* Psalm 34:8	**Blessed**, happiness, how happy; *blessedness*	Psalm 2:12
5479 *chara* James 1:2	**Joy**, cheerfulness, i.e. calm delight: gladness, greatly, (be exceedingly) joy (-ful, -fully, -fulness, -ous)	Romans 15:13

Strong's # and Transliteration:	Definition from Strong's Concordance, unless written in italics:	Use of the word in other Scriptures:
5463 *chaira* 1 Peter 4:13	**Rejoice**, to be "cheerful," i.e. calmly happy or well-off; impersonal especially as, salutation (on meeting or parting), be well: farewell, be glad, God speed, greeting, hail, joy (-fully)	Romans 12:15
3986 *peirasmos* 1 Peter 4:12	**Testing**, a putting to proof (by experiment [of good], discipline or provocation); by implication, adversity: temptation	James 1:2 Hebrews 3:8-9
4137 *pleroo* 1 John 1:4	**Complete**, to make replete, i.e. (literally) to cram (a net), level up (a hollow), or (figuratively) to furnish (or imbue, diffuse, influence), . . . finish (a period or task), verify (or coincide with a prediction), etc.: accomplish, (be) complete, end, expire, fill (up), fulfil, (be, make) full (come), perfect, supply	Philippians 4:19

3.   Look at some of these verses in Psalms 63, 95, and 107 to see what we are called to do and why?

a. Psalm 63:6-8

b. Psalm 95:1-2

c. Psalm 95:3

d. Psalm 107:21

e. Psalm 107:22

4.   Psalm 27:1 is included in Lesson 2, as part of the focus on the comfort we have because of our salvation. In this Psalm of Lament, David shares both his struggle and his faith in his God. Note what David says is his intention in Psalm 27:6.

What does David ask of God in Psalm 27:7-9 and 11-12?

When I read Psalm 27:8-9, I thought of Aaron's "benediction" recorded in Numbers 6:24-26, "The LORD bless you and keep you, the LORD make His face shine upon you and be gracious to you; the LORD lift up His countenance on you and give you peace." How does the teaching in Psalm 27:8-9 and Numbers 6:24-26 challenge you today?

In Psalm 27:14 David testifies twice with the instruction, "wait for the LORD." This word "wait" is the same word used in the promises given in Isaiah 40:31, "those who wait for the LORD will gain new strength; they will mount up with wings like eagles, they will run and not get tired, they will walk and not become weary." OT hope is based on the person of God, as His faithfulness motivates our hope for the future. How does David use the phrase "wait for the LORD" in Psalm 27:14?

5.   Jesus said, "A thief comes to rob, kill, and destroy, but I have come that you might have life and have it in abundance," (John 10:10). I think the thief seeks to rob us of peace and joy, as well as the presence of mind to remember God's word. In the context of John 10:10, Jesus shares two of His "I am" testimonies. What does Jesus say about Himself in John 10:7, 9, and 11?

What does this mean to you?

In Lesson 1, we read David's Psalm 23 where he testifies of God's role in his life and God's character. What is said in the opening verse in Psalm 23 about God?

How does the "divine" Shepherd bring life "in abundance" to you?

6.   The concept of having joy in the midst of trials is taught in James 1:2-5 and this can cause believers to struggle with the sovereignty of God. Think back to the many psalms you have studied that use the words "joy" and "rejoicing." Many of these verses were introduced or are followed by the sharing of struggles and trials.

What does Hebrews 12:1-3 say about Jesus and what does this passage say to those who believe in Jesus as Messiah?

A theme running through Peter's first and second epistles is the concept of "suffering." Peter wrote that we are not to be surprised by the fiery ordeal among us, "which comes for our testing, as though some strange thing were happening to you; but to the degree that you share the suffering of Christ, keep on rejoicing; so that also at the revelation of His glory, you may rejoice with exultation," (1 Peter 4:12-13). Ah, there's the word "rejoice" used twice in v. 13. How can we come to a place where we have "peace" with the truths written in these verses, in other words, how can you consider it all joy when you encounter various trials?

What an amazing blessing we have been given because Jesus shed His blood on the cross as the perfect, complete sacrifice, a sacrifice that never needs to be repeated. Because of Jesus, we have access to God. How is this described in Hebrews 4:14-16?

7.   David shared his testimony in Psalm 63:6-8, "When I remember You on my bed, I meditate on You in the night watches; You have been my help, and in the shadow of Your wings I sing for joy. My soul clings to You; Your right hand upholds me." The phrase "in the shadow of His wings" is used to represent God's tender care and lovingkindness toward His children. (This phrase is also used in Ruth 2:12.)

You have looked at several verses and passages that reflect the attitude of the people of Israel concerning God as the "giver" of joy. Some of God's promises concern specific promises that are the fulfillment of biblical prophecies. God promised He would be faithful to His people after their exile. Earlier you looked at Jeremiah 31 and God's promise of the new covenant. Jeremiah 31:13 declares, "I will turn their mourning into joy and give them joy for their sorrow." Isaiah 35:10, announces, "The ransomed of the Lord will return and come with joyful shouting to Zion, with everlasting joy upon their heads. They will find gladness and joy, and sorrow and sighing will flee away."

I think that Nehemiah 8:10 testifies of the fulfillment of these prophecies in Isaiah 35:10 and Jeremiah 31:13. When I translated the book of Nehemiah from the Hebrew language to English, I wanted to understand the response of the people when they heard God's word read aloud in Jerusalem after they returned from their captivity and exile. I translated Nehemiah 8:10b as, "Do not be grieved, for joy comes from a relationship with the LORD, He is our strength." I really desire to live in this way, regardless of life's circumstances. I ask God to restore my spirit so that when I am not feeling joyful, I might turn to my Father God, my Savior Jesus, and the Holy Spirit for comfort and fellowship, so that my relationship is restored. I long for the joy that comes from a relationship with each member of the Trinity and know that it is a blessing we can know to be true; joy does come from my relationship with the Lord, He is my strength.

Look back at the Psalms you studied in the **Observation Questions** and summarize what is promised and what is asked of us as believers.

I have two favorite hymns that both reflect on the theme of "joy" and I have included both of these here. Close with a time of worship, rejoicing in the joy of the Lord, His peace, His blessings, His faithfulness, His love, and His goodness.

"Like a River Glorious"

Like a river glorious is God's perfect peace, o'er all victorious in its bright increase; perfect, yet it floweth fuller every day, perfect, yet it growth deeper all the way.

Refrain: Stayed upon Jehovah, hearts are fully blest; finding, as He promised, perfect peace and rest.

Hidden in the hollow of His blessed hand, never fee can follow, never traitor stand; not a surge of worry, not a shade of care, not a blast of hurry touch the spirit there.

Refrain:

Every joy or trial falleth from above, traced upon our dial by the Sun of Love. We may trust Him fully all for us to do; they who trust Him wholly find Him wholly true.

Refrain:

By Frances R. Havergal and James Mountain

"Joyful, Joyful, We Adore Thee"

Joyful, joyful, we adore Thee, God of glory, Lord of love; hearts unfold like flowers before Thee, hail Thee as the sun above. Melt the clouds of sin and sadness, drive the dark of doubt away; giver of immortal gladness, fill us with the light of day!

All Thy works with joy surround Thee, earth and heaven reflect Thy rays, stars and angels sing around Thee, center of unbroken praise: Field and forest, vale and mountain, blooming meadow, flashing sea, chanting bird and flowing fountain, call us to rejoice in Thee.

Thou art giving and forgiving, ever blessing, ever blest, well-spring of the joy of living, ocean depth of happy rest! Thou our Father, Christ our Brother – All who live in love are Thine; teach us how to love each other, lift us to the joy divine.

By Henry van Dyke and Ludwig van Beethoven

Day 5 – Concluding Thoughts on God as the Comforter and How We Are to Comfort Others

1.   In our calling as followers of Jesus Christ, we are to glorify our God, which includes the dimension of making known what the Bible says about our Savior, and making known the meaning of truth, love, redemption, faithfulness, power and strength, wisdom, peace, hope, all of which will bring us joy.

A dear friend reminded me one day that when something difficult happens, it is not because our God was asleep. Psalm 121 declares promises revealing God's faithfulness and says of God, "He who keeps you will not slumber. Behold, He who keeps Israel will neither slumber nor sleep," (Psalm 121:3b, 4). In this psalm, the word "keep" can also be translated as "guard," which testifies of God's protection and love for His children. The prophet Habakkuk cried out to God about the troubling circumstances in Israel and his lament in Habakkuk 1:1-4 reveals his brokenness. Habakkuk 1:5 begins God's answer, "Look among the nations! Be astonished! Wonder! Because I am doing something in your days – you would not believe if you were told." God is ALWAYS working, bringing forth His will.

While the Lord is reigning and will reign forever, He is present with us in every moment. God has promised that He will never leave His children. I have been ministered to by this truth and by my God and Savior who faithfully comfort me through His holy word, because God's word is living and powerful and speaks truth. We know that God is on His throne in heaven, and Jesus is seated at His right hand, and yet Scripture proclaims of our God being "near" us. Our God is all-knowing and He is faithful and loving. We cannot forget these two verses from the Psalms: "The LORD is near to the brokenhearted and saves those who are crushed in spirit," (Psalm 34:18) and God "heals the brokenhearted and binds up their wounds," (Psalm 147:3).

Open in **prayer** and begin with these **observation questions**.

➢ This conclusion to our study brings the challenge for you to think about how you can live in obedience to the command in 2 Corinthians 1:4. The fact that you have come to this place in the study means you are probably trusting the Triune God with your own life and living in the provision of the comfort He has for you. A significant component to "accepting" God's comfort is accepting His sovereignty. We have seen the transition between some of the psalmists and prophets who voiced their laments before God in their confusion, frustration, and doubt before coming to a place of acceptance. Later in 2 Corinthians, Paul gives an example of what had brought comfort to the church in Corinth through his disciple Titus. What examples does Paul give concerning the ministry of Titus and the ministry of the church in Corinth in these verses?

a. 2 Corinthians 7:6

b. 2 Corinthians 7:7

c. 2 Corinthians 7:11-16

➤ What are the commands given in 1 Thessalonians 5:14 that would bring comfort to others?

➤ Look at the opening of John's first epistle (1 John 1:1-4), to see what was John's "reason" for his writing according to 1 John 1:4?

➤ Think about what is "commanded" in Romans 12:1-2. What is your "living and holy spiritual sacrifice," according to Romans 12:1 and how is this further described in Romans 12:2?

➤ What is our calling according to Hebrews 12:28-29 and how is this possible and why?

2.   Here are **word studies** for some **key words** in this part of the lesson.

Strong's # and Transliteration:	Definition from Strong's Concordance, unless written in italics:	Use of the word in other Scriptures:
4851 *sumphero* 1 Corinthians 12:7	**Common good,** to bear together (contribute), i.e. (literally) to collect, or (figuratively) to conduce; . . . advantage: be better for, bring together, be expedient (for), be good, (be) profit (-able for)	1 Corinthians 14:26
3619 *oikodome* 1 Corinthians 14:3	**Build up**, see the **word study** for edification in Lesson 5, Days 1 and 2	Romans 14:19
26 *agape* 1 Corinthians 13:1	**Loved**, see the **word study** for love in Lesson 2	John 15:9
25 *agapao* John 15:9	**Love**, see the **word study** for love in Lesson 2	John 3:16

3.   In Matthew 22:36-40 Jesus was asked what is the greatest commandment, and He went beyond the foundational law for the people of Israel and rather than quote from the Ten Commandments, Jesus quoted from Deuteronomy 6:4, saying, "You shall love the Lord your God with all your heart, and with all your soul, and with all your mind," (Matthew 22:37) and then Jesus said the second greatest commandment was to "love your neighbor as yourself," from Leviticus 19:18. The entire Leviticus verse commands Israel, "You shall not take vengeance nor bear a grudge against the sons of your people, but you shall love your neighbor as yourself; I am the LORD." Biblical commands are always important to obey and yet sometimes in our grief, God's commands might be especially difficult. Take some time to paraphrase Jesus' teaching in Matthew 22:37 and the entire message in Leviticus 19:18. (Sometimes putting something into your own words helps you realize where you struggle.)

4.   As believers, we are to live in obedience to the "one another" commands in the NT. Jesus said His disciples are to "love one another" in John 13:34 and 15:12. In the NT epistles, Paul, Peter, James, and John as well as the author of Hebrews explain what it means to "love one another" and to "be at peace with one another" through many "one another" commands. In the Bible study, *Philippians and the Call to Biblical Fellowship*,[27] these commands are studied. Below are the "positive" one another commands in the NT. (Some of the "one another" commands are warnings to not do something to another.) Look at these commands using the phrase "one another" or "each other" to see how the Bible says we are to relate to one another.

---

[27] Jan Wells, *Philippians and the Call to Biblical Fellowship* (Sebastopol, CA: *Sunergos* Bible Studies, 2004).

Think about the challenge of these commands. Underline the key words that relate to how obedience to the command would bring comfort.

Jesus said, "be at peace with one another," (Mark 9:50).

Jesus said, "you ought to wash one another's feet," (John 13:14).

"Be devoted to one another in brotherly love," (Romans 12:10a).

"Give preference to one another in honor," (Romans 12:10b).

"Be of the same mind toward one another," (Romans 12:16).

"Pursue things which make for peace and the building up of one another," (Romans 14:19).

"Accept one another as Christ, accepts us, to God's glory," (Romans 15:7).

"Admonish one another," (Romans 15:14).

"Greet one another with a holy kiss," (2 Corinthians 13:12).

"Serve one another through love," (Galatians 5:13).

"Speak truth to each one with his neighbor, for we are members of one another," (Ephesians 4:25).

"Be kind to one another, tender hearted," (Ephesians 4:32a).

"Forgiving each other," (Ephesians 4:32b).

"Be subject to one another," (Ephesians 5:21).

"Bearing with one another; forgiving one another," (Colossians 3:13).

"Admonishing one another with psalms and hymns and spiritual songs, singing with thankfulness in your hearts to God," (Colossians 3:16).

"Comfort one another with these words [of prophecy]," (1 Thessalonians 4:18).

"Encourage one another; build up one another," (1 Thessalonians 5:11).

"Encourage one another," (Hebrews 3:13).

"Consider how to stimulate one another to love and good deeds," (Hebrews 10:24).

"Not forsaking our own assembling together, . . . but encouraging one another," (Hebrews 10:25).

"Confess your sin to one another," (James 5:16a).

"Pray for one another," (James 5:16b).

"Love one another with a pure heart," (1 Peter 1:22).

"Having compassion, one for another," (1 Peter 3:8).

"Be hospitable to one another without complaint," (1 Peter 4:9).

"Employ your gift in serving one another," (1 Peter 4:10).

"Clothe yourselves with humility toward one another," (1 Peter 5:5).

"Greet one another with a kiss of love," (1 Peter 5:14).

"This is the message which you have heard from the beginning, that we should love one another," (1 John 3:11).

"And this is His commandment, that we believe in the name of His Son Jesus Christ, and love one another just as He commanded," (1 John 3:23).

"Beloved, let us love one another," (1 John 4:7).

"Beloved, if God so loved us, we also ought to love one another," (1 John 4:11).

"The commandment we have had from the beginning, that we love one another," (2 John 5).

The foundation of this study is to accept the relevance of the commands of the Bible in today's world. Stop and ask the Lord who you might reach out to today or this week in a way that demonstrates your love for a "neighbor." A dear friend shared that after going through a very difficult "season," she realized she could still "be useful," even in her grief. She said, "I don't have to focus on myself. God sees everything we are going through. . . Look at what Jesus did for us. We have been given full knowledge in His word and a glimpse of the future. When we know God, we can continue" one day at a time.

Read the context of the parable in Luke 10:30-35 to see Jesus' answer to the question, "Who is my neighbor?" in Luke 10:29.

5.   In 1 Corinthians 12 and 14 Paul teaches about the importance of each person in the church through his teaching about spiritual gifts. What important truths are taught to the church in these verses?

a. 1 Corinthians 12:7

b. 1 Corinthians 12:26

c. 1 Corinthians 14:26

In 1 Corinthians 13, Paul describes the "attitude" necessary for the believer. Between the teaching on spiritual gifts in 1 Corinthians 12 and 14, we read what is necessary for the "common good," that will "build up" and "edify" the body of Christ. 1 Corinthians 13 is called "the love chapter" because of the teaching about the necessity for love, using forms of the Greek word *agape*. How does the Holy Spirit describe the concept of love in 1 Corinthians 13?

The word *agape* in the first century world meant "to want the best for someone" and biblical scholars who have studied the way the word is used in the NT have added the understanding as it is explained by Jesus in John 15. How does Jesus describe love in John 15:9-13? What does Jesus ask of His followers and why?

What does Jesus say in John 15:11 about His joy?

6.   In all circumstances our God is sovereign, and while our God is seated on the throne established in heaven, God's sovereignty is not founded on Him being a distant and uncaring authority. Rather, our God is truthful, He does not lie, and His word reveals His character. God is loving in all situations; God has provided everything we need for our redemption; we are sealed and cannot lose our salvation. God is all wise; His wisdom represents His righteousness,

which is not hidden, but is revealed in His word. God is the giver of peace through His Son, the Prince of Peace. God is our hope and Jesus is the living hope. Our relationship with God brings us joy, as followers of Christ. Jesus modeled His joy by giving of Himself, so that we would be free from our sinful nature and be one with our God.

As Paul said in 2 Corinthians 1:4, we are to comfort others as we have been comforted. Jesus says that His followers who remain in Him will "produce much fruit," (John 15:5) and Paul describes the fruit that is produced by those who remain, abide, and dwell in Jesus. In the context of his teaching, Paul contrasts the "deeds of the flesh" with the "fruit of the Spirit" in Galatians 5. Galatians 5:17 says "the flesh sets its desire against the Spirit." What does Paul say about our salvation in Galatians 5:13-26?

What is the evidence of the Spirit according to Galatians 5:22-23?

What is said in Galatians 5:24-25 that further explains the "fruit of the Spirit"?

How would obedience to the truths in Galatians 5:22-26 make it possible for you to comfort others? (Think back to a time someone reached out to you by demonstrating one of the fruit of the Spirit. It is always a blessing to be the recipient of someone's care as they reach out to you in your time of need.)

Here are some practical guidelines for comforting, encouraging, and building up those who are grieving.[28] Pray and allow the Holy Spirit to lead you to be an encouragement to others.

a. Remember the word "comfort" means to come alongside of someone and "call out," and in the Bible this means, calling out truths from God's word, as that is how God confirms His comfort for His children. As God ministers to our every need, so we can pass along His truths to others in their time of need.

b. Our connections with others must be expressed in loving openness and honesty. We are to "mourn with those who mourn," (Romans 12:15) and not deny or ignore someone's pain.

---

[28] Wells, *Philippians*, Ibid.

We are to be aware of the many different kinds of losses in life that bring grief. "True grief tears apart one's former patterns of life, as well as causes sorrow over the loss of a loved one. Grief is, therefore, a doubly painful experience."[29] We are to help others face their pain so that "no bitter root grows up to cause trouble," (Hebrews 12:15).

c. We must be a safe person and allow grieving people to express their emotions, not holding against them their responses in their pain. Our empathy toward another can soften a heart that is hardened by loss and disappointment. Centuries ago, Plato, the Greek philospoher declared, "The highest form of knowledge is empathy, for it requires us to suspend our egos and live in another's world." Our empathy can help someone who is stuck in anger to acknowledge that because of their "loss," life has changed and life will not "go back to normal" as it was before the loss was experienced.

In thinking about the concept of empathy I thought that sometimes I can only express empathy toward another when I realize truths that Paul expressed in Galatians, as he declared in Galatians 2:19b, 20, "I have been crucified with Christ, and it is no longer I who lives, but Christ who lives in me. The life I now live in the flesh, I live by faith in the Son of God, who loved me and gave Himself for me," (Galatians 2:20). After comparing the deeds of the flesh with the fruit of the Spirit, Paul declares that those who belong to Christ Jesus have crucified the flesh with its passions and desires," (Galatians 5:24). Through Christ's presence and truth, we can empathize with others and bring the comfort with which we have been comforted.

d. We are to pray and encourage a lifestyle following the NEWSTART acronym which includes: sensible *nutrition, exercise,* adequate *water* consumption, being outside in the *sunshine, temperance* in all things, fresh *air* and deep breathing, adequate *rest,* and *trusting* in God for all things. The wounds of loss need time to heal and often fear or uncertainty about the future can consume one's thoughts. We must also acknowledge that sometimes people need to take medication for depression.

e. Allow individuals to grieve over a period of time. After three months the initial shock wears off and reality sets in. In the first year the individual will have gone through special occasions like birthdays and holidays without their loved one. It often takes three years before healing and acceptance can be processed. We cannot rush someone through this process. Do not expect the grieving process to be over quickly, there is no easy solution to the complex issues involved in grief. Encourage the person that has experienced a loss to think of themselves as a survivor, rather than a victim. Help point those who are grieving to turn to the Triune God for the biblical truths that WILL bring comfort.

At the end of the Upper Room Discourse, Jesus told His disciples the reason He spoke to them the message in John 13-16 was so "that in Me you may have peace. In the world you have tribulation, but take courage; I have overcome the world," (John 16:33). This is then followed by the recording of Jesus' beautiful prayer in John 17. Often the circumstances of the world can cause us to forget Jesus' teaching, and this will certainly rob us of peace.

---

[29] Jay E. Adams, *The Christian Counselor's Manual* (Grand Rapids, MI: Zondervan Publishing House, 1973), 283.

In this concluding portion of the lesson, please take time to pour out your heart to the Lord and write your psalm of lament in the Appendix, expressing your thoughts and feelings to God, the God of all comfort. Now turn to the Appendix and express your Psalm of Thanksgiving that can help you have a heart of gratitude.

It is the month of December while I am completing this study and I am hearing beautiful Christmas carols being sung. I was reminded of the phrase "comfort and joy" in the English Christmas carol from the 17th century, "God Rest Ye Merry Gentlemen." The song is based on the Christmas story as recorded in Luke 2:9-20. I have included several of the verses which reflect the author's reminder to us of God's intention, voiced by the angel who appeared to the shepherds, "Do not be afraid; for behold, I bring you good news of a great joy which shall be for all the people, for today in the city of David there has been born for you a Savior, which is Christ the Lord," (Luke 2:10-11). While the word comfort" is not used in the Luke passage, that is how the author of the carol interpreted the angel's "birth announcement."

Another English Christmas carol written by Isaac Watts and George F. Handel in the 18th century is "Joy to the World!" and this opening phrase is followed by the reason the world can have joy: "the Lord is come." You might look at the theological truths declared in the following carol, as it reflects God's promises, the news of the coming of Christ who indeed brought "comfort and joy."

"God Rest Ye Merry Gentlemen"

God rest ye merry gentlemen let nothing you dismay, remember, Christ, our Saviour was born on Christmas day, to save us all from Satan's power when we were gone astray;

Refrain: O tidings of comfort and joy, comfort and joy, O tidings of comfort and joy.

In Bethlehem, in Israel this blessed Babe was born and laid within a manger upon this blessed morn; in which His Mother Mary did nothing but take in scorn.

Refrain:

From God our heavenly Father a blessed angel came and unto certain shepherds brought tidings of the same, how that in Bethlehem was born the Son of God by name.

Refrain:

Samuel Wesley

As you have included this study, know that my prayer for you is that you have come to a place where you have a better understanding of the Triune God and their ministry of comforting those who believe in Christ Jesus as Messiah. May you truly rest in God's comfort and may you be one who comforts others as you are comforted yourself. Peter said of Jesus, by "His divine power we have been given everything required for life and godliness, through the true experiential knowledge of Him who called us by His own glory and goodness, (2 Peter 1:3). We can claim this truth as we assemble with others in the body of Christ and be a blessing to others, in the name of Jesus, our Lord and Savior.

APPENDIX

Personal Psalms of Lament

Lesson 1 - Introduction and Comfort Comes to Us from the Word of Truth

Lesson 2 - God's Comfort Comes to Us from His Love and Redemption

Lesson 3 - God's Comfort Comes to Us from His Faithfulness and His Power and Strength

Lesson 4 - God's Comfort Comes to Us from His Wisdom and Peace

Lesson 5 - God's Comfort Comes to Us from Jesus, the Living Hope Who Brings Us Joy

Gratitude Journal and Psalms of Thanksgiving

Scientific research confirms the value of expressing gratitude. A study in the journal entitled "Spirituality in Clinical Practice" studied people who had had heart damage from a heart attack or years of high blood pressure. They found that after keeping a gratitude journal for two months, those being studied had lower levels of inflammation and better heart rhythms. The Greater Good Science Center (GGSC) at the University of California, Berkeley has studied the positive impact gratitude has upon the human body. Their work has been published as *The Gratitude Project*, with the subtitle: *How the science of thankfulness can rewrite our brains for resilience, optimism, and the greater good*.[30] The Greater Good website offers these four "basic guidelines" for gratitude journaling as follows:[31]

1.) Get into the gratitude groove by writing down five things for which you feel grateful. "The physical record is important – don't just do this exercise in your head. The things you list can be relatively small in importance," assure the experts. "The goal of the exercise is to remember a good event, experience, person, or thing in your life – then enjoy the good emotions that come with it."

2.) Focus on being specific, descriptive, and personal. Digging deep into your feeling of gratitude will provide even more positive perks in your wellness than jotting cursory bullet points.

3.) Write regularly, whether you write every other day or once a week. Ideally set a specific time to journal, then honor (and relish) that commitment.

4.) Savor surprises. Unexpected sources of joy affect us most profoundly, so consider the impromptu wonders you may have experienced in the past few days.

Isn't it interesting that the website is called the "Greater Good," as that is the goal and intention of the spiritual gifts as Paul taught in 1 Corinthians 12. Our question is, how can you maintain a "habit" of gratitude to demonstrate your gratitude around others, especially children, so they can observe our appreciation for the "simple things" in life. Paul was inspired to write, "As you therefore have received Christ Jesus the Lord, so walk in Him, having been firmly rooted and now being built up in Him and established in your faith, just as you were instructed and continue to overflow with gratitude," (Colossians 2:6-7). How can we live in obedience the command to "continue to overflow with gratitude"? The word translated as "overflow" is the Greek *perisseuo* and it has several meanings including the following: to excel in something, to be over and above, to abound, and to be in abundance.

---

[30] Jeremy A. Smith, Kira M. Newman, Jason Marsh, and Dacher Keltner, *The Gratitude Project* (Oakland, CA: New Harbinger Publications, 2020).

[31] GreaterGood.berkeley.edu.

I think that true and sincere gratitude can only come from accepting and surrendering to God's sovereignty. Our God is sovereign, He sits on His throne in heaven and our Savior Jesus sits at His right hand, interceding for us from this throne of grace. We are told in Hebrews 4:16 that when we need help we can come boldly to God's throne of grace and we are promised that He will extend His grace and His mercy upon us. John 1:14 declares Jesus as the word that became flesh and dwelt among humanity, and many beheld His glory, glory as of the only begotten from the Father, and Jesus came to earth making known grace and truth.

Your words of gratitude can also include your thanks for what Jesus will do in the future. Jesus modeled this in John 6:11 when he gave thanks before the "miracle" of feeding the multitude. Jesus prayed and praised God for who He is and what He was going to do.

As you reflect on truths you studied in each lesson, write out your Psalm of Thanksgiving that relates to the truths you studied in the Scriptures presented in the lesson.

Lesson:	Psalms of Thanksgiving:
Lesson 1 - Introduction Theme: Truth Choose verses to help you focus on this theme.	

Lesson:	Psalms of Thanksgiving:
Lesson 2 - Themes: Love and Redemption Choose verses to help you focus on these themes.	
Lesson 3 - Themes: Faithfulness, Power, and Strength Choose verses to help you focus on these themes.	

Lesson:	Psalms of Thanksgiving:
Lesson 4 - Themes: Wisdom and Peace Choose verses to help you focus on these themes.	
Lesson 5 - Themes: Hope and Joy Choose verses to help you focus on these themes.	

Inductive Study Methodology

Inductive Bible Study: Using the Bible as the primary source of information and reading with a purpose by asking relevant questions so that by thorough observation one can accurately interpret, determine eternal principles, and then apply Scripture to all circumstances of one's life. God has spoken in the past and continues to speak to reveal Himself to humanity
Through the prophets as recorded in Scripture
Through His Son Jesus, as the word who came to earth in the flesh
Through the Holy Spirit, who gives to all believers the ability to understand God's word
The Four Components of the Inductive Study Methodology

1. Observation: Seeing what the text says, to gain facts and information
The process of observation is foundational to inductive Bible study
Asking the "5 Ws and an H" questions helps students focus on the obvious

Who?	What?	Where?	When?	Why?	How?
People	Events	Places	Time	Reason or purpose	Means or method

2. Interpretation: Determining what the text means to gain understanding
Looking for information and the correlation in the context of Scripture
Looking at the context, by studying the surrounding words, phrases, sentences, paragraphs, chapters, and the book in which something exists, occurs, or is placed. The author's use of the repetition of ideas or thoughts will also help you discover meaning within the context.

3. Principlization: Determining what eternal truths are being taught to see relevance
Recognizing abiding, timeless truths within the author's propositions, arguments, narration, and illustrations while looking for confirmation in other Scriptures.

4. Application: Conviction as to how the truth applies personally, leading to transformation.
Considering the spirit of the text because a "literal" understanding might have been specific to the historical setting of the audience.

Component of the Methodology	Holy Spirit's Ministry	Man's Response	Product of Component
Observation	Illumination	Reasoning	Facts & Information
To focus on the obvious			
Interpretation	Teaching	Evaluation	Understanding
Done in light of context			
Principlization	Conviction	Summarization	Eternal Principles
To seek biblical relevancy			
Application	Guidance	Accountability	Transformation
Begins with individual			

Step 1 - Book Overview: To Discover the Context or the Big Picture of the Book

Purpose: To identify the flow of thought that ties the book together and identifies the author's reason for writing

A. Who is the author?
> Who is writing and what does he say about himself?
> What are his circumstances?
> Where is he and why is he there?
> When in his life is he writing?
> Why is he writing?

B. Who is or who are the recipient/s?
> Who is it written to?
> How is the recipient described?
> What does it say about the recipient?
> What is the relationship of the recipients to the author?
> Where is the recipient?
> Why is the author writing to the recipient?

C. Other people mentioned: (either specifically, or by generalization or implication)
> Who are the other people mentioned and what does the text say about them?
> What do you learn about their relationship to the author or recipient?
> What is their relationship to the key message?

D. Look for key words
> Words generally repeated throughout the text
> When removed the text is left without meaning

E. Look for declarative statements
> Teaching doctrinal truth that would inform and equip those who follow after Christ
> Historical narrative, sharing historical events or personal testimony

F. Look for instructions or commands
> A command or imperative statement, telling someone what they are to do
> Usually written in the second person such as you, your, or yourself; or introduced with the phrase "let us"

G. Look for exhortations
> A personal message from the author to encourage the recipients regarding their own situation, whether personally or within their church
> Show the uniqueness of the situation that led to the book being written
> Sometimes introduced with the word "you," calling or urging obedience

H. Look for admonitions
> Confronting the behavior of the recipient that has not honored God
> To advise strongly, to reprove, or to call the recipients to repentance

I. Look for warnings
　　　To put on guard or to put on notice concerning possible danger, evil, or harm
　　　To describe a just recompense or a possible consequence for behavior based on God's prophecy concerning judgment

Step 2 - Comprehensive Chapter Study: Observation Chapter by Chapter

Purpose: To examine the details of the chapter, to see how the chapter details relate to the book

A. Marking key words
　　　Mark so your eye can see on the page the occurrence of the word
　　　This is typically done with colored pencils
　　　God, Jesus Christ, the Holy Spirit, and their pronouns are always keywords
　　　The key words become a basis for developing a list of facts

B. Making lists of the key words by writing phrases and sentences

C. Reasoning through the lists of information from the key words

D. Contrasts to see differences in perspective
　　　Point out differences in words or phrases
　　　Most contrasts are identified by the following words: but, however, or never the less

E. Comparisons to see similarities in concepts
　　　Dealing with ideas or bodies of truth that are similar
　　　Identified by the words like and as

F. Terms of expression
　　　Time dimension and verb usage
　　　Look for words like now, then, or later
　　　Tells if something occurred in the past, will occur in the future, or is in the present

G. Conclusion or results or purpose
　　　Look for words like: for, for this reason, so that, that, or because

Step 3 - Word Studies

Purpose: To deepen and clarify understanding of the text, To determine the meaning of unknown or confusing words or sections of texts

A. Choose a word
　　　Look at the key words in the text
　　　Look at the words with unclear meanings
　　　Look at the verbs and nouns in the text

B. Look up the definition in a word study tool
　　　A concordance:

Strong's Exhaustive Concordance includes a dictionary of Hebrew and Greek words and their definitions
Expository Dictionaries
Vine's Dictionary of the New Testament
Spiros Zodhiates, Complete Word Study Dictionary of the New Testament
Spiros Zodhiates, Complete Word Study Dictionary of the Old Testament

C. Read the definition back into the text

Step 4 - Cross Referencing of Scripture

Purpose: To establish the context within the broader context of Scripture (Context always rules in all interpretation).
>To amplify or clarify the understanding of the text
>Scripture is the best interpreter of Scripture
>Scripture never contradicts Scripture

A. How to determine cross references:
>Look up the word in a concordance
>Look up the word in a topical Bible
>Look up verses identified by marginal references

B. Read the cross reference

C. Evaluate the message in the light of the cross reference

Step 5 - Determining Paragraph and Chapter Theme and Book Title

A. Paragraph analysis
>Determine the paragraph theme. The editors of some translations of the Bible have each verse starting on a new line within each chapter. The NASB begins each new paragraph by printing the verse number in bold type. The NIV divided the chapters into paragraphs, as we know them, indenting at the beginning of each new paragraph. When you study the ancient languages of the Bible, there are differences in paragraph divisions from one manuscript to another. The words of Scripture were inspired however, it was in the 1300s that verse numbers, paragraph divisions, and the divisions made by chapter numbers were added.

B. Developing each chapter theme and the book title
>Determine a summary statement for each chapter and one for entire book, verified from key words, instructions, exhortations, admonitions, and warnings within the chapter
>Use five words or less, with at least one actual word found in a chapter
>Each chapter title should be descriptive of what is in the chapter and distinctive from the other chapter titles

Place these themes on the **Theme and Title Chart**

Inductive Study Methodology: Summary of the Process

	Step 1	Step 2	Step 3	Step 4	Step 5
What?	The Overview: To discover the context or the big picture of the book	Comprehensive Chapter Studies	Word Studies	Cross Referencing Scripture	Paragraph and Chapter Theme and Book Title
Why?	• To identify the author's reason for writing • To identify the flow of thoughts which ties it together	• To examine the details of the chapter • To examine how the chapter details relate to the book	• To deepen the under-standing of the text • To clarify the under-standing of the text	• To establish the context within the broader context of Scripture • To amplify or clarify the text	• To determine the paragraph and chapter themes • To determine the book title
	A. Author B. Recipient(s) C. Other people D. Key words E. Declarative Statements F. Instructions G. Exhortations H. Admonitions I. Warnings	A. Marking key words B. Contrasts C. Comparisons D. Terms of expression of time, conclusion or results	A. Choose a word in the text B. Read the definition of the word from a dictionary back into the text	A. Look up the word or phrase using: • A concordance • A topical Bible • Marginal references B. Read the cross reference C. Evaluate the message in the light of the cross reference	A. Summary statements for each paragraph, chapter, and the book based on the key words, declarative statements instructions, exhortations, admonitions, and warnings Use five words or less Each chapter title should be distinctive from the other chapter titles, descriptive of what is in the chapter B. Place each theme on the Theme and Title Chart

Word Studies

OT Words (in Hebrew)

A
Abundance 7320   31
Almighty 7706   56

B
Blessed 835   87

C
Comfort 5162   13
Comfort 5165   12
Compassion 7356   31
Confidence 4009   80
Covenant 1285   31

E
Establish 3559   73

F
Faithful 539   49
Faithfulness 530   49
Favor 5278   73
Fear 3374   49, 65
Forgive 5545   37
Forgive 5546   37
Forgiveness 5547   37

G
Good 2896   24
Grief 2490   44

H
Hope 2342   81
Hope 3176   80
Hope 8615   80
Hosts 6635   56
Humble 6031   60

I
Insight 2449   64

J
Joy 2304   87

L
Lament 5091   24
Lament 5594   24
Lamentation 5092   24
Lord 113   80
Love 157   31
Love 160   30
Love 2836   30
Lovingkindness 2617 30

M
Mercy 2603   31
Mercy 7356   10, 81
Most High 5945   44
Mourning 6937   56

P
Peace 7965   69
Praise 8416   60
Praiseworthy 8416 31
Promise 1697   49

R
Redeemed 1350   37
Redemption 6304   37
Rejoice 8055   87
Remember 2142   19
Revive 2421   13

S
Salvation 3444   37
Save 3467   37
Sing for joy 7442 87
Soul 5315   60
Strength 1369   56

T
Thank 3034   24, 60
Thanksgiving 8426 24, 60

Trust 982	49		J	
Truth 571	18		Joy 5479	88
U			L	
Upholds 8551	49		Lament 2354	24
			Lamented 3602	24
W			Love 25	31, 94
Wait 3175	81		Love 26	31, 94
Wait for 6960	37, 56		Loved 26	91
Wise 2450	64			
Wisdom 2451	64		M	
Word 1697	19		Mercy 1656	31
Words 565	19		Mercies 3628	12
			Mourn 3996	13

NT Words (in Greek)

			P	
B			Peace 1515	69
Build up 3619	94		Power 1411	56
			Promises 1860	49
C			Promises 1862	49
Comfort 3870	12			
Comfort 3874	12		R	
Common good 4851	94		Redemption 629	37
Complete 4137	88		Rejoice 5463	88
Covenant 1242	31		Release 859	37
			Remember 3403	19
E				
Edification 3619	81		S	
Encouragement 3874	81		Sorrows 3077	13
			Strength 1412	56
F			Strengthen 4599	57
Faith 4102	49			
Faithful 4103	49		T	
Forgive 863	37		Testing 3986	87
			Thanksgiving 2169	25
G			Truth 225	19
Grace 5485	25, 31			
Grief 3076	13		W	
Grief 4727	13		Weep 2799	13
			Wisdom 4678	65
H			Wise 4680	65
Helper 3875	12		Word 3056	19
Hope 1680	81			
Hoped 1679	81			

Bibliography

Adams, Jay E. *The Christian Counselor's Manual.* Grand Rapids, MI: Zondervan Publishing House, 1973.

Bauer, Walter, William Arndt, Frederick W. Danker, and F. W. Gingrich. *A Greek-English Lexicon of the New Testament and Other Early Christian Literature.* Chicago, IL: University of Chicago Press, 2000.

Brown, Francis, Samuel Rolles Driver, and Charles Augustus Briggs. *Enhanced Brown-Driver-Briggs Hebrew and English Lexicon.* Oxford, UK: Clarendon Press, 1977.

GreaterGood.berkeley.edu

Gunkel, Herman and J. Begrich. *Introduction to the Psalms: The Genres of the Religious Lyric of Israel.* Translation J. D. Nogalski; Macon, GA: Mercer University Press, 1998.

Henslin, Earl and Becky Johnson. *This Is Your Brain on Joy.* Nashville, TN: Thomas Nelson, 2008.

Howard, David M. Jr. "Praising God in the Bad Times," 1991.

Kaiser, Walter C. Jr. "Promise." In *Holman Bible Dictionary.* Nashville, TN: Holman Bible Publisher, 1991.

Keller, Phillip. *A Shepherd Looks at Psalm 23.* Grand Rapids, MI: Zondervan Publishing House, 1982.

Kiuchi, Nobuyoshi. *Leviticus.* Nottingham, UK: Apollos, 2007.

Lewis, C. S. *The Problem of Pain.* London, UK: The Centenary Press, 1940.

Smith, Jeremy A., Kira M. Newman, Jason Marsh, and Dacher Keltner. *The Gratitude Project.* Oakland, CA: New Harbinger Publications, 2020.

Strong, James. *The Comprehensive Concordance of the Bible.* Iowa Falls, IA: Word Publishing.

Tucker, W. D. *Dictionary of the Old Testament: Wisdom, Poetry and Writings.* Tremper Longman III and Peter Enns, editors. Downers Grove, IL: IVP Academic, 2008.

Weiser, Artur. *The Psalms.* Philadelphia, PA: Westminster Press, 1962.

Wells, Jan. *1 Peter, An Inductive Bible Study.* Sebastopol, CA: *Sunergos* Bible Studies, 2020.

Wells, Jan. *Philippians, and the Call to Biblical Fellowship, An Inductive Bible Study*. Sebastopol, CA: *Sunergos* Bible Studies, 2003.

Zodhiates, Spiros. "Lexical Aids to the Old Testament." In *The Hebrew-Greek Key Study Bible*. Chattanooga, TN: AMG Publishers, 1990.

Sunergos Bible Studies

	Number of Lessons:
Inductive Studies:	
Joshua and the Call to Live Victoriously by Faith	10
The Book of Ruth	4
The Life of David	12
The Book of Nehemiah	8
The Book of Esther	5
Jonah	10
The Sermon on the Mount (Matthew 5 – 7)	14
The Gospel According to Mark	22
The Epistle to the Romans	23
Galatians and the Fruit of the Spirit	10
Ephesians	12
Philippians and the Call to Biblical Fellowship	12
Colossians	9
Titus and the Call to Biblical Discipleship	9
Philemon (Learn the Inductive Bible Study methodology with this short study)	2
The Epistle to the Hebrews	16
James	11
1 Peter	9
2 Peter	6
Jude	4
Revelation 1 – 5	6
Survey Study:	
Introduction to the New Testament	13
Topical Studies:	
Biblical Holiness and the Call to Be Holy	9
Knowing the God of All Comfort	5
Old Testament Worship for Followers of Christ	8
Prayers of the Bible	12
Women of the Word	12
Discipleship Series Studies: Each lesson is like one day's work in the other studies	
The Call to Following Jesus the Messiah	10
The Call to Biblical Character – An In-depth Look at the Beatitudes (Matthew 5:3-12)	11
The Call to Bear Fruit by the Power of the Spirit – Galatians 5:22-23	12
The Call to Live Victoriously by Faith – Ephesians 6:10-20	10
The Call to Biblical Fellowship – An In-depth Look at the "One Another" Commands	12

Made in the USA
Monee, IL
11 September 2023

42502555R00070